High Scorer's Choice Series

IELTS 5 Practice Tests

General Set 5

(Tests No. 21-25)

High Scorer's Choice Series, Book 10
IELTS 5 Practice Tests, General Set 5 (Tests No. 21–25)
ISBN 9780648000075
Copyright © 2019 Simone Braverman, Robert Nicholson.
First Edition June 2019
Updated June 2020

Available in print and digital formats
Accompanying audio recordings to be downloaded on the following webpage:
https://www.ielts-blog.com/ielts-practice-tests-downloads/

All rights reserved. No part of this work (including text, images, audio or video content) may be reproduced or transmitted in any form or by any means, electronic or mechanical, including photocopying, recording or any information storage and retrieval system without permission in writing from the authors.

IELTS® is a registered trademark of University of Cambridge ESOL, the British Council, and IDP Education Australia, which neither sponsor nor endorse this book.

To contact the authors:
Email: simone@ielts-blog.com
Website: www.ielts-blog.com

Acknowledgements

The authors hereby acknowledge the following websites for their contributions to this book (see the webpage below for a complete list):

www.ielts-blog.com/acknowledgements/

In memory of Peter, our wonderful narrator, whose voice accompanied thousands of IELTS test takers on their journey to success.

While every effort has been made to contact copyright holders it has not been possible to identify all sources of the material used. The authors and publisher would in such instances welcome information from copyright holders to rectify any errors or omissions

Praise for
High Scorer's Choice Practice Tests

"I am a teacher from Australia. I had a Chinese friend who is studying for the exam and I used these [tests] to help him. I think the papers are very professional and useful. Many of the commercial practice papers are not culturally sensitive but this was not a problem with your tests."
- *Margaretta from Australia*

"I found out that your practice papers are excellent. I took my IELTS on March 11th and got an Overall Band 8 with listening – 8, reading – 9, writing – 7 and speaking – 7. I spent one month on preparation."
- *Dr Yadana from London, UK*

"I must tell you that the sample tests I have purchased from you have been the key to my preparation for the IELTS. Being employed full time I do not have the time to attend classes. I downloaded the material and made myself practice a few hours every 2 or 3 days for 3 weeks and was successful on my first trial. I was able to get an average of 7.5 and I was aiming at 7."
- *Oswaldo from Venezuela*

High Scorer's Choice IELTS Books

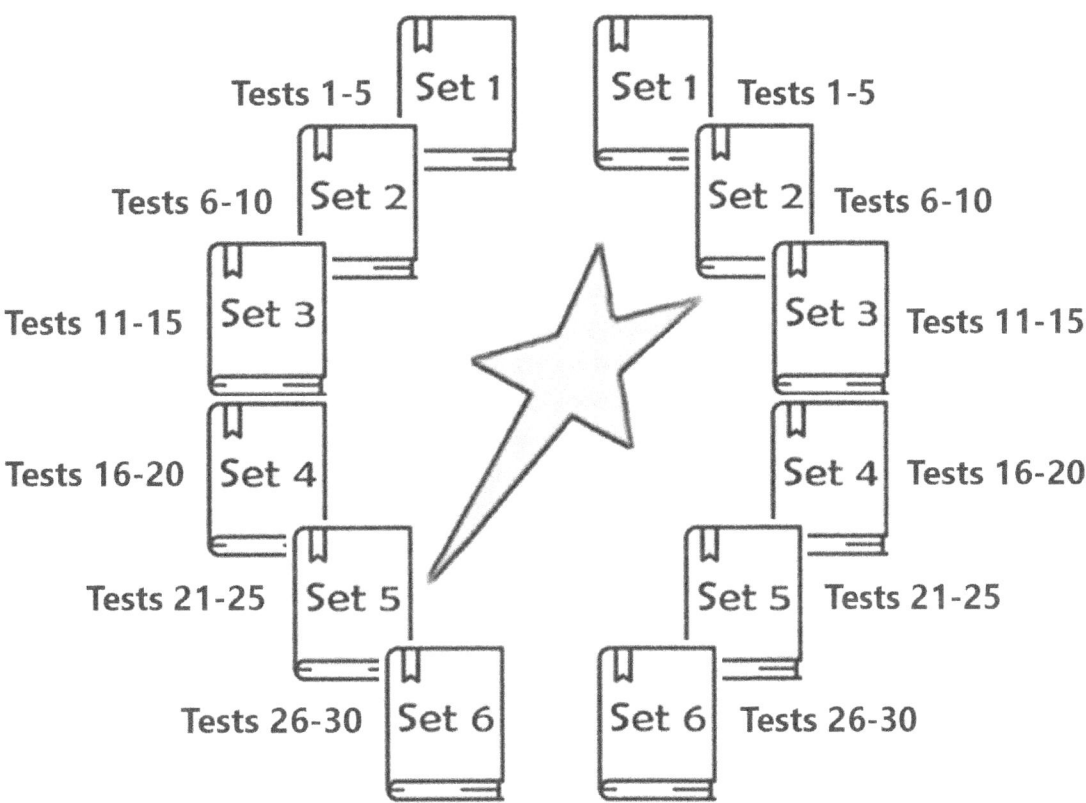

CONTENTS

How to prepare for IELTS	…………………………………………	5
Practice Test 21	…………………………………………	7
Practice Test 22	…………………………………………	26
Practice Test 23	…………………………………………	46
Practice Test 24	…………………………………………	68
Practice Test 25	…………………………………………	89
Blank Answer Sheets	…………………………………………	111
Answers	…………………………………………	112
Reading Answers Help	…………………………………………	115
Example Writing Answers	…………………………………………	130
Speaking Examiner's Commentary	…………………………………………	136
Listening Transcripts	…………………………………………	144

Download Audio Content

In order to download the audio content please use a desktop computer (not a mobile device) with a reliable internet connection and open the following webpage in your browser:

https://www.ielts-blog.com/ielts-practice-tests-downloads/

Follow instructions on the webpage to save all audio files on your computer. The files are in mp3 format and you will need an audio player to listen to them (any modern computer has that type of software preinstalled).

How to prepare for IELTS

There are two ways for you to use these practice tests for your exam preparation. You can either use them to work on your technique and strategy for each IELTS skill, or you can use them to simulate a real exam and make sure you will do well under time pressure.

| Option 1 | **Use practice tests to work on your IELTS skills (no time limits)** |

To prepare well for the IELTS exam you need to have a strategy for each sub-test (Listening, Reading, Writing and Speaking). This means knowing what actions to take, and in which order, when you receive a test paper. If you are working with the IELTS self-study book "Ace the IELTS – How to Maximize Your Score", all the necessary tips are located in the book. You need to read and then apply these tips and techniques when you are practicing on some of these tests. Don't time yourself, concentrate on learning the techniques and making sure they work for you.

If you purchased the practice tests in digital format, you will need to print out some pages, for easier learning and to be able to work in the same way as in the real test (on paper). Print the Listening questions and the Reading passages and questions. You can read the Writing and Speaking questions from your computer or mobile device, to save paper and ink. If you have the paperback format, this doesn't apply to you. Use Table of Contents on the previous page to navigate this book.

If Listening is one of your weaker skills, use transcripts while listening to recordings, when you hear words or sentences that you don't understand. Stop the recording, rewind, locate in the transcript the sentence you had a problem with, read it, and then listen to the recording again.

If Reading is hard for you, after doing the Reading test use the Reading Answer Help section of these practice tests to understand why the answers in the Answer key are correct. It will show you the exact locations of the answers in the Reading passages.

To compare your own writing to high-scoring samples go to Example Writing Answers and read them. Note the way the information is grouped and the tone (formal/informal) used in Writing Task 1, and the way an essay is organised in Writing Task 2.

To practice in Speaking, either read to yourself the Speaking test questions or get a friend to help with that. Record your answers and then listen to the recording. Note where you make long pauses while searching for the right word, pay attention to your errors and your pronunciation. Compare your own performance to that of students in sample interviews, and read their Examiner's reports.

| Option 2 | **Use practice tests to simulate the real test (strict time limits)** |

This option will require some prep work before you can start a simulated test. Print out or photocopy the blank Test Answer Sheets for Listening and Reading and prepare some ruled paper on which to write your Writing Task 1 and 2. Also, think of a way to record yourself in the Speaking sub-test. Get a watch, preferably with a timer. Allocate 3 hours of uninterrupted time.

1. Be in a quiet room, put the Listening questions in front of you and start playing the recording. Answer questions as you listen, and write your answers next to the questions in the book.

2. When the recording has finished playing, allocate 10 minutes to transfer all your Listening answers to the Listening Answer Sheet. While you are transferring the answers check for spelling or grammatical errors and if you missed an answer, write your best guess.

3. Put the Reading passages and questions in front of you and set the timer to 60 minutes. Begin reading passages and answering questions. You can write the answers next to the questions or straight on the Answer Sheet. Remember that you don't get extra time to copy answers to the Answer Sheet, and that when 60 minutes are up all your answers must be written on the Answer Sheet.

4. Put the Writing questions in front of you and set the timer to 60 minutes. Make sure you don't use more than 20 minutes for Task 1, including proofreading time, and that you don't use more than 40 minutes for Task 2, with proofreading included.

5. Put the Speaking questions in front of you and begin the interview (remember to record your answers). In Part 2 take the whole 1 minute to prepare your speech and make notes, and then try to speak for 2 minutes (set the timer before you start talking).

6. When you have finished the whole test, take some time to rest, as you may be tired and it may be hard for you to concentrate. Then check your answers in the Listening and Reading against the correct ones in the Answer key, compare your writing tasks to the Example Writing tasks and your recorded speaking to the example interview. Analyse and learn from any mistakes you may find, and especially notice any problems with time management you may have encountered.

   Remember, it is OK to make mistakes while practicing as long as you are learning from them and improving with every test you take.

   Good luck with your exam preparation!

PRACTICE TEST 21

LISTENING

Download audio recordings for the test here:
https://www.ielts-blog.com/ielts-practice-tests-downloads/

SECTION 1　　Questions 1 – 10

Questions 1 – 5

Complete the form below.

*Write **NO MORE THAN THREE WORDS AND/OR A NUMBER** from the listening for each answer.*

<table>
<tr><td colspan="2" align="center">Gresham Garage
New Job Details</td></tr>
<tr><td>Customer's Name:</td><td>(**1**) _____ Clarke</td></tr>
<tr><td>Address:</td><td>18 Green Lane
Cranford</td></tr>
<tr><td>Postcode:</td><td>CR8 (**2**) _____</td></tr>
<tr><td>Telephone:</td><td>Home:　Not given
Work:　Not given
Cell:　07538 (**3**) _____ 983</td></tr>
<tr><td>Bill Payment Method:</td><td>(**4**) _____</td></tr>
<tr><td>Work Details:</td><td>Problem with the (**5**) _____.</td></tr>
</table>

Questions 6 - 9

Complete the summary below.

*Write **NO MORE THAN TWO WORDS AND/OR A NUMBER** from the listening for each answer.*

Work on Mr. Clarke's Toyota

Mr. Clarke left the car at the garage and so he got a taxi to take him home. The last service was approximately (**6**) _____ months ago, so he booked a service at the garage. He mustn't forget the car (**7**) _____ when he goes to pick up the car. Mr. Clarke or his wife can pick the car up on (**8**) _____ 26th. The service costs (**9**) _____ pounds (including all the work the car needs) plus parts. The garage will ring Mr. Clarke if they need permission for any unexpected or expensive work.

Question 10

*Choose the correct letter **A, B or C**.*

*Write the correct letter in box **10** on your answer sheet.*

10   How did Mr. Clarke initially find out about Gresham garage?

    A   Some friends of his told him
    B   An advertisement in a newspaper
    C   Online

SECTION 2   Questions 11 - 20

Questions 11 – 15

Answer the questions below.

Write **NO MORE THAN THREE WORDS** from the listening for each answer.

11   Who is the principal audience for the hospital information talk?

12   Which document will give the telephone number of an inpatient's ward?

13   For what reason are scheduled beds not sometimes available?

14   How are pre-admissions assessments usually conducted?

15   What should inpatients give to the nurses after arriving at the hospital?

Questions 16 and 17

Choose the correct letter **A, B, or C**.

16   All people staying overnight at the hospital must

    A   wear hospital nightclothes.
    B   bring their own towels.
    C   bring books to read.

17   Computers are permitted in the hospital, but

    A   not e-books, as they can affect hospital equipment.
    B   people will have to pay a small fee for charging them.
    C   people have to use headphones.

Questions 18 - 20

Label the plan below.

Write **NO MORE THAN THREE WORDS** from the listening for each answer.

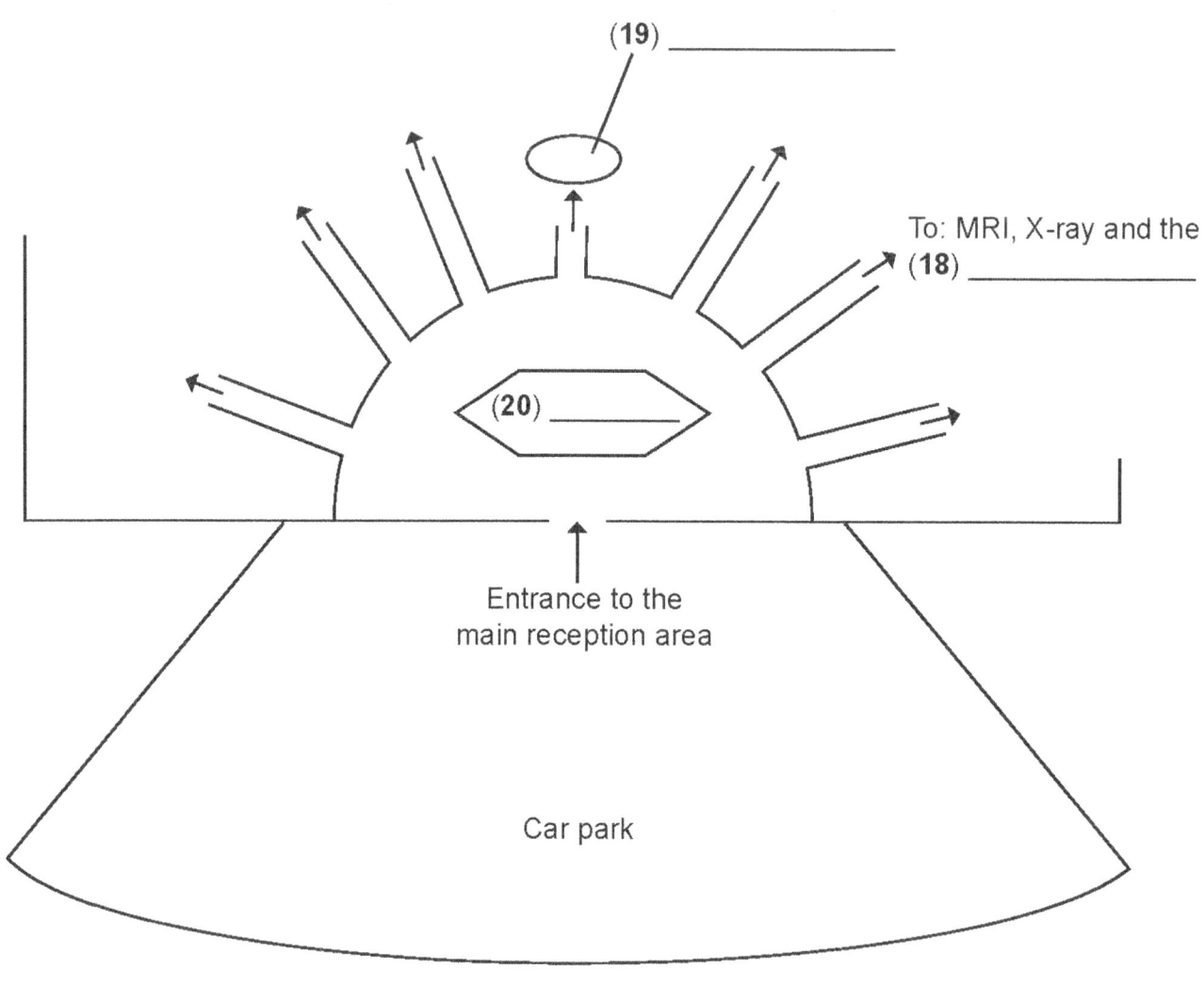

SECTION 3   Questions 21 – 30

Questions 21 – 25

Answer the questions below.

Write **NO MORE THAN THREE WORDS AND/OR A NUMBER** from the listening for each answer.

21   What geological feature from millions of years ago is it thought Lake Baikal resembles?

22   Lake Baikal is located in what type of geographical formation?

23   What is found between the bottom of the water in Lake Baikal and the rock of the lake's bottom?

24   What proportion of animal life found in Lake Baikal is unique to the region?

25   What do Lake Baikal's seals have more of that allows them to swim underwater for more than 70 minutes?

Questions 26 – 30

Complete the table below.

Write **NO MORE THAN TWO WORDS** from the listening for each answer.

Lake Baikal			
Climate	Lake Baikal is warmer in winter than the rest of southern Siberia due to the size of the lake.		
Temperature		Lake Baikal	Rest of Siberia
	Mid Winter Temperature	- 21 °C (average)	- 90 °C (lowest)
	Summer (August) Temperature	11 °C (average)	16 °C (average)
	The lake is frozen from January - May / June. In August, the lake's mean (**26**) _____ is on average 10 - 12 °C.		
Water Quality	Lake Baikal is very clear as it contains few (**27**) _____. The clarity is helped by plankton that eat debris. (**28**) _____ is available all through the lake, even at the bottom.		
Water Sources	Water enters Lake Baikal from the Selenga River in the south east + 300 other sources. The Angara River is the sole (**29**) _____ in the south west. Because of the lake's low temperatures, only relatively little water is lost through (**30**) _____.		

SECTION 4   Questions 31 – 40

Questions 31 – 40

Complete the notes below.

*Write **NO MORE THAN TWO WORDS** from the listening for each answer.*

The Siberian Tiger

Largest sub-species of tiger.
Location - south-eastern Russia + northern China.

- 1940's - 1960's - danger of extinction due to hunting (only approx. 40 tigers in wild).
- Russia was the first to give the tiger total (**31**) _____ + the Cold War closed the tigers' forest environment.
- 1980's - approx. five hundred tigers in wild.
- Soviet Union's collapse led to poaching and the devastation of the tigers' (**32**) _____ (this led to only approx. 450 tigers left in the wild at that time).
- Conservation + anti-poaching has now led to a stable population of approx. 450 tigers in wild.
- Originally found in the boreal forests of Russian Far East, China + Korean peninsula.
- Now only in Russian Far East + border areas of China and North Korea.
- Northern boreal forests are (**33**) _____ with coniferous trees (spruce, fir, and pine).
- Bordered by tundra in the north and steppes in the south.
- Extremely cold - The (**34**) _____ creates long winters with little sun - temperatures can be minus 45 °C.
- The Siberian tiger is protected from the cold by very thick fur and lots of (**35**) _____.
- Poaching to supply tiger parts for Chinese medicine leads to many tigers being killed - there is a belief that tiger parts can treat diseases and rejuvenate the body.
- Specialists from the west have rejected the (**36**) _____ of tiger parts.
- Habitat loss is also a significant threat - this has also led to a lack of the tigers' (**37**) _____.
- The reduced tiger numbers have also led to a lack of (**38**) _____, which makes successful breeding a problem. This also has weakened the tigers' (**39**) _____, so that the tigers are very vulnerable to illness.
- Various stakeholders are taking action to preserve the Siberian tiger.
- The most important element in the Siberian tiger's conservation is to plan (**40**) _____ that everyone must embrace.

READING

SECTION 1   Questions 1 – 14

Questions 1 – 7

*There are 5 advertisements **A – E** on the next page.*

*Answer the questions below by writing the letters of the appropriate advertisements in boxes **1 – 7** on your answer sheet.*

1   Which advertisement is for a place that has recently expanded?

2   Which advertisement states that items sold are subject to strict rules?

3   Which advertisement offers a special option for Monday lunchtimes?

4   Which advertisement states that customers have to be registered before they can buy?

5   Which advertisement says a reservation is advisable?

6   Which advertisement states that the business is run according to ecological principles?

7   Which advertisement states that improvements will soon be made?

A Tradewise Cash and Carry

Specialising in wholesale supplies to shops, restaurants and other businesses.

To trade at Tradewise Cash and Carry, you must be a business or a charity. Membership is free. All customers must be over 18. An email address is required to complete your registration. Your account details will be sent to this email address once the online registration process is complete. Check our website for further details: www.tradewise.com

B Ted's Fish and Chips

Eat in or takeaway, you can enjoy our traditional fish and chips 7 days a week, 11.00 - 22.00.

Lunchtime specials available
    Mon - Fri, 11.00 - 14.30

Free delivery for orders over £15.

Please note that from 13th November we'll be closed for one week for renovations.

C Stanbourne Farmers' Market

A trip to our fabulous farmers' market is the best way to find high quality food that reflects the character and diversity of the area. Discover, browse and sample a wide variety of local foodie delights from fruit and vegetables straight from the garden to freshly baked pies, bread, organic meats and plenty of other treats. The freshness and taste of locally grown food is unbeatable! The producers at our farmers' market have to meet specific criteria, so that you can be assured of authentic high quality produce. Local really does mean local – all the produce must be grown, reared, caught or processed by the stall holder and all within a 30-mile radius of the market.

D Bilat's Convenience Store

Store opening hours are:
    Monday to Friday 07.00 - 18.00
    Saturday 08.00 - 13.00
    Sunday 08.00 - 12.00

We are an independent and family-run store selling groceries and household goods, with a focus on ethical and environmental practices. You'll find items such as fresh bread, soft drinks, newspapers and magazines, fresh vegetables, confectionery, household products, frozen foods and much more. We also have additional items of course that suit our local community. You can be assured that all the items available are of the finest quality and value.

E The Happy Taco - Mexican Restaurant

Come and enjoy the wonderful tastes of Central America! Everything on our menu is authentic Mexican food made from scratch by our experienced Mexican chefs.

- Free drink with any meal, Tuesday to Thursday!
- Check out our new extension!
- Mexican and salsa music on Friday and Saturday nights with dancing!

Booking recommended!

Open: Tuesday - Sunday   12.00 - 15.00 *(lunch deals available)*
                                             17.30 - 23.30
Closed on Mondays

Questions 8 – 14

Complete the sentences below.

Write **NO MORE THAN TWO WORDS** from the text for each answer.

Write your answers in boxes **8 - 14** on your answer sheet.

8   Joining the Glendowen Photography Club requires filling in the _____ available on the website.

9   New members will get a _____ after the relevant payment.

10   Club competitions are assessed by an _____.

11   A _____ governs the yearly improvement of members' photographic skills.

12   The _____ ensures that membership of the club committees is rotated.

13   Various _____ can be found within each forum.

14   There must be _____ of a new member's joining before they will receive emails.

The Glendowen Photography Club

We are a group of like-minded individuals who have got together to share our passion for photography.

The Glendowen Photography Club welcomes new members with any level of experience. Many prospective members start by visiting the club for a meeting or two to help them decide whether they would enjoy participating. All our meetings are open to visitors. We gather twice a month on Monday nights at 7.30 in the Glendowen Community Centre. Applying for membership is easy. Download and print the nomination and lodge it with one of the committee members. Annual fees are currently sixty dollars (or pro rata for half a year if you join after June). Also required is a once-only joining fee of twelve dollars that covers the costs of the joining pack.

The club conducts monthly competitions with six categories open to all members. The rules prescribe a set topic for each month and open entries, where you choose the subject of the pictures, are also invited. We also have separate Monochrome and Altered Reality/Creative sections. An independent judge scores and provides feedback on all entries. Through the club's monthly competitions, a member's work is evaluated alongside that of other members. After each competition entry is assessed, constructive comment is provided on its merits. The standard of members' photographic output is therefore constantly increasing as they learn more, correct faults and strive harder to compete.

Among the club's key objectives is the ongoing education of its members. Our syllabus is designed to extend and challenge members' talents and abilities. Workshops are also held regularly. These cover subjects of interest to members ranging from technical matters to talks on interesting themes. Regular excursions also provide amazing informal learning opportunities. Being an active participant in a vibrant photography club like ours is a certain way of continually expanding your understanding of picture taking and presentation of images.

As well as a central committee that helps run the club, we also have separate sub-committees, which help spread the organisational and bureaucratic load. According to our constitution, all the posts on the club's committees have to change regularly and so we're always looking for committed, creative and flexible candidates who want to do their bit for the club.

Our website hosts various forums, which allow members to discuss items of interest from their homes or phones. Inside each forum there can be different categories related to the forum topic, which start with an initial statement or question posted by a user. Other users add replies, extending the conversation. All of our forums are restricted to members only and will not appear unless you are logged in. You must be logged in to create a topic or reply. Report any inappropriate postings to the forum moderator, whose email address can be found on all the forum pages.

Our "Photo News" email list is one of the primary means for keeping club members informed of club activities and events. To subscribe, please send an email request to the email administrator (address found on the website). After verification of your club membership, your email address will be added to the distribution list, and you will receive a welcome message via email. The club does not share member information with 3rd parties, nor will we send out any messages not directly related to club business.

SECTION 2   Questions 15 – 27

Questions 15 – 21

Do the following statements agree with the information given in the text?

In boxes 15 – 21 on your answer sheet write:

TRUE   *if the statement agrees with the information*
FALSE   *if the statement contradicts the information*
NOT GIVEN   *if there is no information on this*

15   Companies have to show a good reason for the monitoring of employees.

16   Some businesses may be obliged to monitor their employees.

17   Employee monitoring policies should be available on company websites for everyone to access.

18   Companies are permitted to prohibit employees from accessing certain websites while at work.

19   Companies don't have to inform employees why they're being monitored if CCTV is used for this.

20   An employee having his or her bag searched should ask the union representative to be present.

21   It is illegal to secretly monitor employees.

Monitoring Employees

Employers may wish to monitor their workplace for various reasons. Although the law doesn't prevent employers from monitoring workers, employers should remember workers are entitled to some privacy at work. Employers must tell employees about any monitoring arrangements and the reason for it. Key points relating to monitoring are:
- Employers should have written policies and procedures in place regarding monitoring at work.
- Monitoring shouldn't be excessive and must be reasonably justified.
- Staff should be told what information will be recorded and how long it will be kept.

Monitoring in the workplace can occur for a variety of reasons; it can be used to safeguard employees, i.e. to ensure workers aren't at risk from unsafe working practices. In some sectors, employers may have a legal or regulatory need to carry out some monitoring. The information gathered through monitoring should only be used for the purpose it was carried out for, unless it leads to the discovery of other things, such as a breach of health and safety. Employers may monitor staff at work in various ways. This can include web monitoring, CCTV, bag searches and covert monitoring.

Web Monitoring

Although employers don't have to allow workers the use of phone, e-mail or Internet for personal matters, many employers will allow some access as long as it doesn't interfere with their work. If employers do monitor this use, the workers should be clearly informed and given the reason why it will be carried out. Employers should have procedures in place setting out what is and isn't allowed. Some websites may be banned or marked as at risk. Employers should tell workers if they are being monitored, what counts as a reasonable amount of personal emails and phone calls and if personal calls and emails are not allowed. These procedures should be made clear and understood by all workers. If a worker does not comply with the policy and procedures, they may be liable to disciplinary action.

CCTV Monitoring

CCTV monitoring can be used in the workplace for a number of reasons, however, if CCTV is installed, the employer should make sure the employees are aware of it. This is usually done by displaying signs to say where the locations of the cameras are. Workers must also be given the reason for the monitoring. Signs should be clear, visible and readable, contain details of the purpose of the surveillance and who to contact about the scheme, and include contact details such as website address, telephone number or email address.

Bag Searches

If employers intend to carry out bag searches, a workplace policy must be in place that informs employees that bags and purses will be subject to searches. Employers must have a legitimate work-related reason for carrying out searches.

Covert Monitoring

It's very rare that employers would need to carry out covert monitoring without the staff being told they are being monitored, but they can do it. Employers must have a genuine reason to carry out covert monitoring, such as criminal activities or malpractice. Monitoring must be obtained as quickly as possible, and only as part of a specific investigation.

Questions 22 – 27

Choose **SIX** letters, **A - J**.

According to the text, what can you do to gather information on competitors?

Write the correct letter, **A - J**, in any order in boxes **22 - 27** on your answer sheet.

A   Become an actual customer with your competitors.

B   Read relevant advertising by competitors.

C   Read published material on your competitors.

D   Spread rumours about your competitors with your own customers.

E   Ask a friend to gather material for you from competitors' offices.

F   Conduct Internet searches on competitors' merchandise.

G   Question your own customers to see if they have information on competitors.

H   Ask old employees of your competitors about them.

I   Question your own suppliers to see if they have information on competitors.

J   Interact with your competitors when appropriate.

The Competition

Knowing who your competitors are, and what they are offering, can help you improve your products, services and marketing. It will enable you to set your prices competitively and help you to respond to rival marketing campaigns with your own initiatives. You can use this knowledge to create marketing strategies that take advantage of your competitors' weaknesses, and improve your own business performance. You can also assess any threats posed by both new entrants to your market and current competitors. Remember that competition is not just another business that might take money away from you. It can be a potential product or service that's being developed that you should start selling or license before somebody else takes it up. Your competitor could be a new business offering a substitute or similar product that makes your own redundant – keep an eye out on advertising, which is where this information often appears. This knowledge will help you to be realistic about how successful you can be.

Try to find out as much as you can about your competitors. Look for articles or adverts in the trade press or mainstream publications. Read their marketing literature. Check their entries in directories and phone books. If they are an online business, ask for a trial of their service. If your competitor is a public company, read a copy of their annual report. Limited companies have to lodge their accounts with Companies House.

At exhibitions and trade fairs, check which of your competitors are also exhibiting. Look at their stands and promotional activities. Note how busy they are and who visits them. Look at competitors' websites. Find out how they compare to yours. Check the site to see if you could use aspects of it to improve your own website. Is their information easy to find? Business websites often give much information that businesses haven't traditionally revealed - from the history of the company to biographies of the staff. They may provide case studies on customer success stories. Sign up to your competitors' email newsletters to keep track of their business news, like new customers or product launches. Use a search engine to track down similar products. Find out who else offers them and how they go about it.

You can learn about your competitors by getting to know them. Phone them to ask for a copy of their brochure. You could ask for a price list or enquire what an off-the-shelf item might cost and if there's a discount for volume. This will give you an idea at which point a competitor will discount and at what volume. Phone and face-to-face contacts will also give you an idea of the style of the company, the quality of their literature and the initial impressions they make on customers.

Make the most of contacts with your customers. Ask which of your competitors they buy from and how you compare. Use your judgement with any information they volunteer. For instance, when customers say your prices are higher than the competition, they may just be trying to negotiate a better deal. Use meetings with your suppliers to ask what their other customers are doing.

At the same time as competing, make sure that you are competing fairly and do not behave in an anti-competitive fashion. Fixing prices or agreeing not to compete is illegal.

It's also likely you'll meet competitors at social and business events. Talk to them. Be friendly - they're competitors, not enemies. You'll probably share common problems. You'll get a better idea of them - and you might need each other one day, for example in collaborating to grow a new market for a new product.

SECTION 3 Questions 28 – 40

Read the following passage and answer Questions 28 – 40.

Oceanic Dead Zones

Dead zones are areas of water bodies where aquatic life cannot survive because of low oxygen levels. They begin to form when excess nutrients, primarily nitrogen and phosphorus, enter coastal waters and help fertilise blooms of algae. The major nutrient sources are fertilisers, sewage, and the burning of fossil fuels. When these algae die and sink to the bottom of the sea, they provide a rich food source for bacteria, which in the act of decomposition consume dissolved oxygen from the surrounding waters. This decomposition also breaks them down to nutrients again, continuing the cycle. If stratification of the water column prevents the mixing or dissolution of atmospheric oxygen into these waters, the deleted areas will remain oxygen poor. Shallow waters are much less likely to stratify compared to deep waters, and are thus less liable to develop hypoxia. First, shallow waters tend to be well-mixed by winds and tides, and second, waters that are shallow and clear enough to allow light to reach the bottom can support primary oxygen producers such as phytoplankton, algae, and seagrasses that release oxygen during photosynthesis. The darkness of deeper water prevents phytoplankton from producing the required oxygen. As the situation worsens, more and more oxygen is used up until all organisms die, and a dead zone is formed.

Dead zones are primarily a problem for bays, lakes and coastal waters, since they receive excess nutrients from upstream sources. About half of the hypoxic zones around the world are seasonal, as oxygen depletion occurs in spring and summer following the increase in phytoplankton that results from nutrient enrichment. These hypoxic zones usually last from a few weeks to several months; however, in some locations, about 8 per cent of worldwide hypoxic conditions occur continuously throughout the year. The size of these hypoxic zones can vary significantly from year to year.

As human populations increase and the land suffers further degradation, requiring more and more fertiliser, dead zones will become more commonplace. For example, every year now, near where the Mississippi River goes into the sea, large dead zones form of 22,000 square kilometres. These areas are totally devoid of fish and other life except for anoxic bacteria. Farming using excessive nitrogen fertilisers in the river's catchment area is blamed for this and a plan has been formulated to reduce dead zones by 30 per cent over the next 3 years.

When some types of algae blooms are large and produce chemicals, or toxins, the event is called a harmful algal bloom. Harmful algal blooms can occur in lakes, reservoirs, rivers, ponds, bays and coastal waters, and the toxins they produce can be harmful to human health and aquatic life. Harmful algal blooms are mainly the result of a type of algae called cyanobacteria, also known as blue-green algae. These harmful algal blooms release toxins that contaminate drinking water, causing illnesses for animals and humans. After being consumed by small fish and shellfish, these toxins move up the food chain and can hurt bigger animals like sea lions, turtles, dolphins, birds, manatees, and fish. Even if algal blooms are not toxic, they can hurt aquatic life by obstructing the sunlight and clogging fish gills.

Algal blooms and dead zones also have less obvious effects. Economists have examined the effects of nutrient overenrichment on both market goods, primarily commercial fisheries, and nonmarket industries, primarily recreational. Although many aquatic ecosystems have yet to be properly studied in this regard, there is plenty of research that shows how much impact dead zones have had on these two economic spheres. For example, it's been recently shown that there would be considerable benefits in terms of the economy to reducing nitrogen loading and hypoxic conditions in the Baltic Sea, which is an area that has long suffered dead zones caused by these problems. It has been suggested that reducing dead zone areas in the Baltic could be valued at about 10 billion dollars.

A more fundamental effect of hypoxia is the loss of energy from the ocean. By precluding or stunting the growth of bottom-dwellers such as clams and worms, hypoxia robs their predators of an important source of nutrition. For example, scientists estimate that Chesapeake Bay in the United States loses about 10,000 metric tons of energy to hypoxia each year, 5 per cent of the Bay's total production of food energy. The Baltic Sea has lost 30 per cent of its food energy – a condition that has contributed to the significant decline in its fisheries' yields.

Dead zones are a key stressor of marine ecosystems and rank with over-fishing, habitat loss, and harmful algal blooms as global environmental problems. They take a toll on the economy, hurting industries and sectors that depend on clean water. In addition, federal, state and local governments spend billions of dollars per year to combat nutrient pollution or prevent its effects. In order to improve the situation, a variety of action is required, including regulatory programs, the education of the various areas of society that are in any way involved and the provision of support, including financial commitments, to ensure that the programs and education takes place effectively and successfully.

Questions 28 – 30

Label the diagram below. Write **NO MORE THAN ONE WORD** from the text for each answer.

Write your answers in boxes **28 - 30** on your answer sheet.

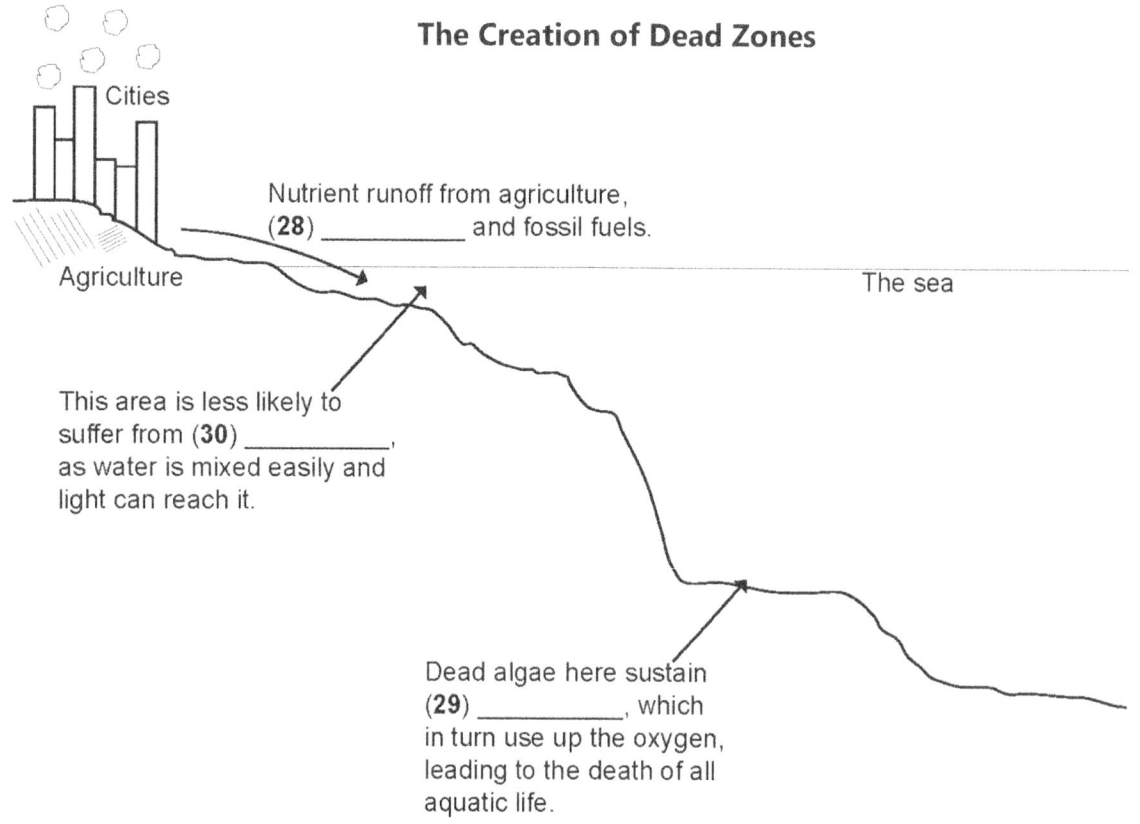

Questions 31 – 40

Complete the notes below.

Write **NO MORE THAN TWO WORDS** for each answer.

Write your answers in boxes **31 - 40** on your answer sheet.

Oceanic Dead Zones

- Many oceanic areas suffer from dead zones; they can be permanent or (**31**) _____. The size varies.

- With more (**32**) _____ of agricultural land, there will be more dead zones like the ones at the mouth of the Mississippi River. Nitrogen pollution from the (**33**) _____ of the river has created very large dead zones.

- Harmful algal blooms can pollute drinking water and can make animals sick. As the toxins are absorbed into this water and the (**34**) _____, larger animal and humans can be affected. In the sea, the blooms can block both the sun and (**35**) _____.

- Dead zones also affect market and nonmarket goods, in the business and (**36**) _____ sectors. (**37**) _____ already illustrates the effects and the (**38**) _____ of improving the economic situation in various areas.

- (**39**) _____ is also taken from the oceans by dead zones by removing food. The Chesapeake Bay and Baltic Sea have been studied in this regard.

- Dead zones have various negative effects and a lot of money is spent on controlling them.

- New laws, (**40**) _____ of important stakeholders and resources are required to make a positive difference.

WRITING

WRITING TASK 1

You should spend about 20 minutes on this task.

You recently went to a lecture that you very much enjoyed.

Write a letter to the organiser of the lecture. In your letter,

- **explain that you really enjoyed the lecture and why**
- **ask for details of the lecturer, so you can contact him/her in person**
- **suggest another lecture topic for the future**

You should write at least 150 words.

*You do **NOT** need to write any addresses. Begin your letter as follows:*

Dear Sir / Madam,

WRITING TASK 2

You should spend about 40 minutes on this task.

Write about the following topic:

The number of advertisements for charities on television and the Internet seems to be increasing.

What is causing this? Is this a positive or a negative development?

Give reasons for your answer and include any relevant examples from your knowledge or experience.

You should write at least 250 words.

SPEAKING

PART 1

- What kinds of things do you eat for dinner in your country?
- What fruits and vegetables are popular in your country?
- Where do people buy their food in your country?

Topic 1   Cities

- What is your favourite city? (Why?)
- What are the advantages and disadvantages of living in a city?
- Can a city be beautiful? (Why?/Why not?)
- How can we reduce pollution in cities?

Topic 2   Friendship

- Who are your best friends?
- What are some of the qualities a good friend should have?
- Why do people need friends?
- Are friends more important than family? (Why?/Why not?)

PART 2

Describe an animal that you particularly like.
You should say:
  what this animal is
  when and where you see this animal
  what this animal does when you see it
and explain why you particularly like this animal.

PART 3

Topic 1   Animals

- In what ways do animals help people?
- Why have the numbers of wild animals decreased so much over the last 50 years?
- What things can we do to conserve wildlife?
- Do you think it is acceptable to test cosmetics on animals? (Why?/Why not?)

Topic 2   Zoos

- What are the good things and bad things about zoos?
- Do you think governments should fund zoos? (Why?/Why not?)
- How do you think zoos will change over the next 30 years?
- Do you think it's right to spend so much money on keeping animals in zoos when there are so many people suffering from poverty? (Why?/Why not?)

PRACTICE TEST 22

LISTENING

 Download audio recordings for the test here:
https://www.ielts-blog.com/ielts-practice-tests-downloads/

SECTION 1　　Questions 1 – 10

Questions 1 – 10

Complete the summary below.

Write **NO MORE THAN THREE WORDS AND/OR A NUMBER** *from the listening for each answer.*

Dominic's Interview

A young man came for an interview today as a new beach cleaner. His name is Dominic (**1**) _____. He gave his address as 34 Queens Crescent in Stanmore and the post code is ST5 932. His date of birth is the second of September (**2**) _____. He gave his national insurance number, which is FL 63 (**3**) _____ 2 H, but he didn't have a P45, as he's lost it. He gave his mobile phone number as 07535 391 288 and he doesn't mind using it at work, as he has (**4**) _____ as part of his phone contract. Dominic would prefer to be paid (**5**) _____ every week.

Dominic will work 7 days a week, from (**6**) _____ a.m. to 9 a.m. and 7 p.m. to 10 p.m., though he might be late in the evening of Thursday due to a lecture - alert his (**7**) _____. He will travel by (**8**) _____ to where he is on duty for cleaning every day. Dominic must wear (**9**) _____ when cleaning the beach to protect himself and he must hand in any (**10**) _____ that he finds while cleaning.

SECTION 2   Questions 11 - 20

Questions 11 – 14

Choose the correct letter **A, B, or C**.

Write the correct letter in boxes **11 - 14** on your answer sheet.

11   Why is the museum café closed?

   A   It is being renovated.
   B   It experienced a fire.
   C   The café has now been permanently replaced by vending machines.

12   The guide phones can be used

   A   on payment of a small fee.
   B   without cost.
   C   on payment of a small returnable deposit.

13   How often is the film on Australian canals shown?

   A   Every 10 minutes.
   B   Every 20 minutes.
   C   Every 30 minutes.

14   Feedback should be

   A   left in the box by the exit.
   B   given on the museum's website.
   C   emailed to the museum.

Questions 15 – 20

Match the canal (questions **15 - 20**) with the statement.

Choose **SIX** letters from the box below, **A - H**, and write them on the answer sheet.

15   The Berry Canal

16   The Clarke Canal

17   The Alexandra Canal

18   The Cook Canal

19   The Hawthorne Canal

20   The Sale Canal

	Statements
A	This canal used to be a small river.
B	This canal's operations were disrupted, because the canal became too shallow.
C	This canal was never used for the purpose for which it was built.
D	This canal was built as a result of someone dying.
E	This canal is made up of two waterways for craft to travel in different directions.
F	This canal's construction was halted, because of a lack of funds.
G	This canal no longer has water in it.
H	This canal's construction was of interest to archaeologists.

SECTION 3   Questions 21 – 30

Questions 21 – 26

Complete the table below.

*Write **NO MORE THAN TWO WORDS** from the listening for each answer.*

The Psychology Course	
Year 1	A sound basis of psychological theory and analysis. Lots of (**21**) _____ in Behavioural Neuroscience.
Year 2	In depth study of Cognitive Psychology and Perception, Developmental Psychology and Social Psychology. (**22**) _____ will still be studied.
Year 3	More Clinical Psychology. Specialisations - (**23**) _____ Psychology, Clinical Psychology, Educational Psychology, Social Psychology, Developmental Psychopathology, Forensic Psychology, Perception + more. Students can study two (**24**) _____ not related to psychology.
Job Prospects	Students can be professional psychologists or enter other professions. The course's (**25**) _____ involve a reasoned approach, problem solving and the handling and management of data – these can help in a variety of careers. The understanding of people's (**26**) _____, and the ability to deal with and fix problems is also a plus in lots of industries.

Questions 27 – 30

Complete the sentences below.

*Write **NO MORE THAN TWO WORDS** from the listening for each answer.*

27   Students will need to choose a topic and then find a _____ from the teaching staff of the Psychology department.

28   A _____ can be obtained if a student's research paper is judged as being the best.

29   A lot of _____ in students is needed as well as reading and research in order to do well in the research paper.

30   An important part of the research paper is the _____, where students need to analyse previous studies on their subject.

SECTION 4 Questions 31 – 40

Questions 31 – 38

Complete the notes below.

*Write **NO MORE THAN THREE WORDS** from the listening for each answer.*

Pollution and the UK Aviation Industry

- Last year's figure of over 200 million passengers in UK airports arrested a **(31)** _____ of air industry figures. **(32)** _____ show this rise will continue by 25% over 5 years and 50% over 10 years.
- Good air traffic numbers affects a variety of economic sectors, but the noise and air pollution can negatively affect people's **(33)** _____.
- The noise from aircraft is proportional to **(34)** _____ and originates from the moving parts of aircraft.
- Aircraft engine emissions pollute the air and, in spite of good engine efficiency, increased air travel is making the situation worse - this is also aggravated by **(35)** _____.
- ICAO has now set limitations on various emissions from jet engines and the expelling of **(36)** _____. Aircraft engines have also had lower emissions due to new technologies.
- UK government targets for CO_2 emissions are threatened by aviation growth, the effects of emissions at altitude and the lack of an **(37)** _____ for current fuels.
- A programme of improved technology, better operational practice and demand management is addressing the issue in the UK. To be effective, **(38)** _____ is necessary and the UK government should adopt a leading European role in developing solutions.

Questions 39 and 40

Complete the diagram below.

Write **NO MORE THAN THREE WORDS AND/OR A NUMBER** from the listening for each answer.

Black Carbon Measurements of Passenger Aircraft

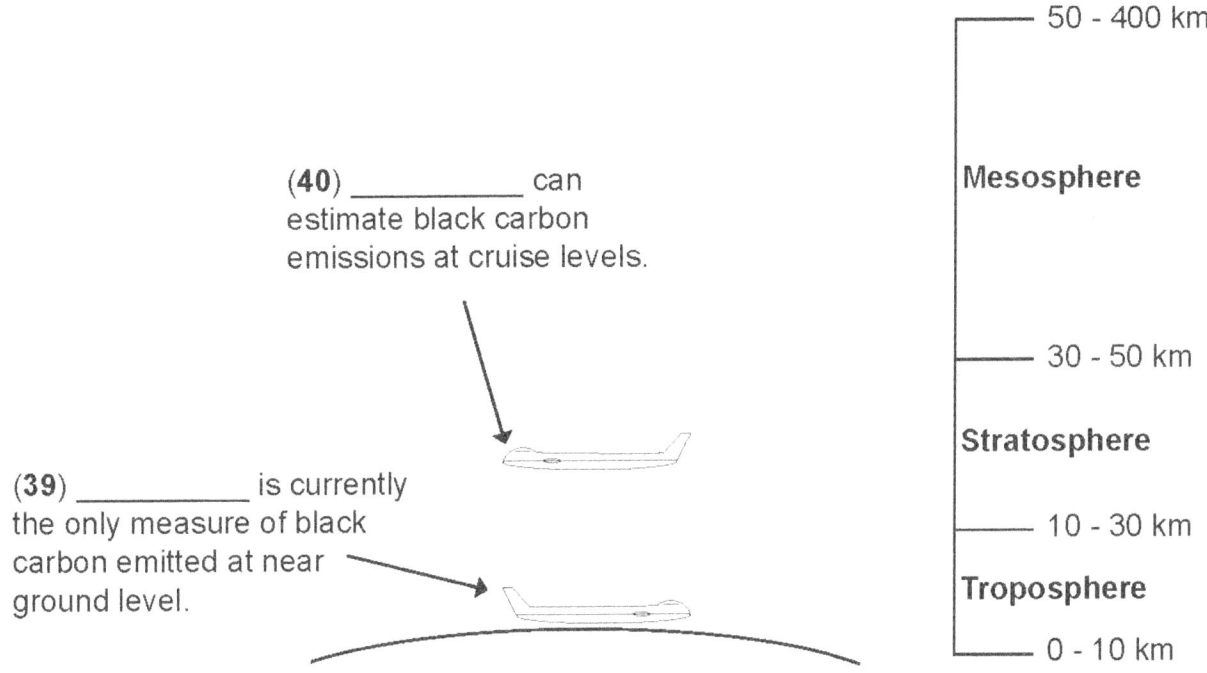

READING

SECTION 1 Questions 1 – 14

Questions 1 – 7

Answer the questions below.

Write **NO MORE THAN THREE WORDS** from the text for each answer.

Write your answers in boxes **1 - 7** on your answer sheet.

1 What document outlines the philosophy of the Busy Bees After School Club?

2 With what assistance can young children at the Infants School go safely to the Busy Bees After School Club?

3 Where can children at the Busy Bees After School Club read quietly on their own?

4 Who will help new children get used to being at their first day at Busy Bees Weekend Club?

5 What must children bring with them if they attend the Busy Bees Weekend Club?

6 What can parents take advantage of if they book early for the Busy Bees Weekend Club?

7 With whom should parents communicate regarding when to drop off and pick up their children after trips organised by the Busy Bees Weekend Club?

Busy Bees After School Club

At Busy Bees After School Club, we provide a well-equipped secure environment within which your child can participate in a wide range of activities. The club policy ensures that the enthusiastic, fun and caring approach to the needs of your child will create a safe and enjoyable experience. All our enthusiastic staff participate in continual training, both on the job and in the classroom, which they then bring back to inspire policy and practice updates. We do a lot of in-house training to ensure everyone is working to the same high standards. All our staff either have childcare qualifications or are working towards them. Our recruitment standards are high, and we do thorough and extensive checks before employment. Parents interested can read recommendations and parents' stories on our website.

An integral part of child development is about building confidence, and giving children opportunities to explore the world around them, to learn about themselves and others in a safe, caring environment. This is at the core of everything we do. We treat each child as a unique individual and with equal respect, encouraging them to treat each other in the same way. We seek to meet their particular needs built on their talents and interests, act as advocates for their right to play and therefore enhance their experience at the club.

For $15 a day, the Busy Bees After School Club provides a safe, secure and caring environment for children aged from 4 to 11, from the end of school at 3 p.m. until 5.45 p.m. We are based in the new Sports Pavilion at the town's Junior School, with a walking service offered for the children who attend the local Infants School. We have a selection of toys and games and there are arts and crafts activities based on a weekly theme. The children also have the opportunity to do cookery activities on most days and there is colouring, painting, competitions, word searches and plenty of other developmental games. In addition, we have a chillout zone where the children can chat and read comics. A choice of fresh fruit, healthy snacks and different fruit juice drinks are available each day. The latter part of the session consists of games/sport and outside play during the warmer and lighter periods of the year. All children are encouraged to take part in team games or individual play.

We also provide childcare for children aged 4 and above during the weekend and offer a wide range of fun play activities and outings. When you first come into the Weekend Club, you and your child/ren will be greeted by a member of the team who will ask you to sign your child in and welcome them to the session. The boards in the reception area will highlight the activities that your child will be participating in on that day. Please sign your child's name in the correct book (under 8 – Yellow; Over 8s- Blue; 11 Plus- Green) and the Playworker looking after your group will take your child into the play area and help them settle in (especially on their first day). Please check if there is any additional permission forms, for face painting for example. If you have any queries or have additional information to give us, please let us know. We provide snacks consisting of fruit and fruit juice; children should please bring lunch.

Early bookings help us to plan more exciting trips and activities and we would like to encourage you to take advantage of the discount rate by doing this. Any booking made 20 days or fewer prior to the start date of the Holiday Club will be $5 extra.

Times: Weekend Club, 8.00 a.m. – 5.45 p.m. (Breakfast is served between 8.00 a.m. and 8.30 a.m. at no extra cost). Children can arrive and depart at any time during the day except trip days, when we ask that children arrive no later than 9.00 a.m. and parents should liaise with the Club Leader regarding estimated collection times. On many trips, we are booked in at a particular time that we have to strictly adhere to - being late can make us miss our booking.

Questions 8 – 14

Do the following statements agree with the information given in the text?

*In boxes **8 – 14** on your answer sheet write:*

> **TRUE**   *if the statement agrees with the information*
> **FALSE**   *if the statement contradicts the information*
> **NOT GIVEN**   *if there is no information on this*

8   The museum traces Australian maritime history back over a thousand years.

9   Virtual tours are available for educational establishments.

10   A certain amount of the museum can be visited without cost.

11   Guided tours of the museum can be arranged for a minimum of 7 visitors.

12   Extreme weather limits the range of the museum sights that can be visited.

13   The museum will be closed for a limited time due to renovations.

14   All food consumed at the museum must be purchased inside the museum.

The Australian National Maritime Museum

The Australian National Maritime Museum is Australia's national centre for maritime collections, exhibitions, research and archaeology. As Sydney's most visible national cultural institution, we are committed to connecting audiences right across Australia in both urban and regional areas. From our base, the museum presents a changing program of stimulating exhibitions and events to share Australia's maritime history and connect the stories, objects, people and places that are part of our country's narrative. Our permanent and temporary exhibitions and our National Maritime Collection explore and represent Australia's close links to the sea covering Indigenous Australian's deep connection to ocean, early exploration, immigration, commerce, defence, adventure, sport, play and identity.

The museum offers over 30 workshops and tours across a number of curriculum areas. Run by qualified and experienced teacher guides, sessions are imaginative and hands-on and suitable for students from year one to university level. Many schools can attend from their classrooms via the latest digital technology.

Admission

Tickets are available to purchase online or on arrival at the museum. Pre-book online to beat the queues.

Gallery Ticket — Explore for free our permanent galleries showcasing the best of the museum's collection.

Big Ticket — The Big Ticket is our best-value deal. Enjoy unlimited access to everything open at the museum on the day of your visit. This includes entry to all exhibitions and activities, all our action experience stations, our moored vessels, hands-on arts and craft activities in Kids on Deck, under-5s play zone Mini Mariners Play and our 3D Cinema, where you can see our various specialist films. 20% discount on Big Ticket prices for groups of 10 or more only with ahead bookings (see website).
- NOTE: Children must be taller than 90cm to go onboard the vessels and on hot days we close all vessels when the temperature reaches 36° Celsius to ensure visitor safety.

Led by highly knowledgeable volunteer guides, the museum offers guided tours of our world-class vessel fleet, exhibitions and collections. Ask at museum's reception on the day. If you would like to request a guided tour for your group, please book online at least 2 days in advance. NB: Guided tours are subject to availability. Before you visit, download our App, which includes video tours and information that brings the Maritime Museum to life. It's free, and constantly being updated.

We're upgrading our visitor experience during February when the museum will be undergoing renovations. Our foyer will be temporarily closed for February, with our ticket office relocated to the side of the museum closest to Murray Street. Our staff will be available to help you find your way. We apologise for any inconvenience and look forward to welcoming you soon with an upgraded visitor experience. Other areas affected include the 3D theatre and the Mini Mariners Play Space.

Buy healthy and delicious food at the museum's café or takeaway kiosk or bring your own picnic lunch to eat on the museum's harbour-side terrace. Our café offers relaxed, open-air café dining with spectacular views of the harbour. Enjoy lunch, sunset drinks or a simple snack. Dine in or takeaway.

SECTION 2   Questions 15 – 27

Questions 15 – 21

Complete the summary using the words in the box below.

Write your answers in boxes **15 - 21** on your answer sheet.

Planning a Website for your Business

Failing to plan can lead to (**15**) _____ when the actual construction takes place and so planning well can save time. Pinpointing the (**16**) _____ of the site early can provide direction, so make a record of what you want. Research the (**17**) _____ and begin to decide exactly who to target. Consider your site's content and its location. Be aware of (**18**) _____ you might have to abide by. Be very specific with product information, as this will help with search engine optimisation. Make your website easy to navigate and make use of accepted design (**19**) _____ to make your website user friendly. Make sure your website is completely on-brand, but don't sacrifice (**20**) _____ for this. Bear in mind that many/most people access websites through mobile devices and you may require a responsive website or even a separate mobile website – remember your website's (**21**) _____ may depend on this aspect of design!

accessibility	location	purpose
regulations	competition	misunderstandings
conventions	advice	professionals
ranking	factors	legalities

Planning a Website for your Business

Constructing an effective website without a plan is like constructing a building without blueprints. Things end up in the wrong place, features are overlooked, and the situation is ripe for miscommunication between website developer and client. Planning your website ahead of time will give it clear direction as well as prevent missed deadlines and backtracking.

Because planning is so essential when it comes to designing a website, start by identifying the exact rationale for having a site. Typical reasons why businesses develop websites include building brand awareness, finding new customers, saving money, selling products and providing improved customer support. We recommend that you write down what you want to do with your website. What are your goals and what features would you like to see on your website? For example, you can write down the things you'd like to include: have a blog section, photo gallery, online store, reservation system and contact form. If you are unsure about what you want, then check out companies working in the same sector as you or other websites for inspiration. Once you establish what you want your website to accomplish, look at your prospective audience. This can include your current and potential customers, new prospects, stakeholders, suppliers and partners.

Decide on the type of content you will need to support the objectives of your site and how to present this online. Think about balancing the amount of text, images and interactive content that you wish to publish on your site. Also, think about where you place elements on the page. For example, marketing messages or 'calls to action' may be more effective if placed 'above the fold'. This refers to the area of the page that is immediately visible once the page has loaded and before the user has scrolled down the page in the browser window. When you are planning content for your site, don't forget you are legally required to publish certain company information. If you are creating an e-commerce website, provide unique descriptions for your products or services. This will help with search engine optimisation and ensure that you stand apart from your competitors.

The key to designing a successful website is understanding the needs of your audience and reflecting these in your design. Don't make users navigate through too many layers of the site to find the information they want. Provide clear navigation aids, so the user can quickly find the information they need. A standard navigation bar that is in the same place on every page enables the user to move quickly through the site. Follow established web practices for navigation - this will help make your website more intuitive for the user.

If you already have a recognisable brand or image, make sure to incorporate it into your design. Your website should reinforce your corporate brand, use your company logo consistently throughout the site and be part of your wider marketing strategy in an attempt to reach your target audience. While you are making sure that your website is consistent and true to your brand, don't forget - it also needs to be easy to use.

When you design your website, you need to consider how it will look and work on mobile devices. More and more users are upgrading to new smartphones and tablet computers, which they use to browse and search the Internet. Search engines now grade content based on how well it appears on mobile devices. Although your website will be viewable on mobile devices, a more effective mobile presence may call for a separate mobile website or a responsive design. Mobile-first approach is a popular strategy that involves designing for the smallest screen first and working your way up. The thinking behind this is that, if your website is good on a mobile device, it will translate well on all other devices, including desktop.

Questions 22 – 27

There is some information on negotiating with business energy providers, **A – F,** on the next page.

Which section of information mentions the following advice?

Write the correct letter, **A - F**, in boxes **22 - 27** on your answer sheet.

22 Be selective of exactly when you want to start your contract.

23 Take into account any projected changes in your business before deciding on a contract length.

24 Ask your energy company whether you can get a reduced payment for prompt payment.

25 Negotiating a contract length that can allow you to take advantage of lower prices is an important consideration.

26 Tell your energy company about when you use the most energy.

27 It's important to consider whether there are costs to leave a contract when you think about changing provider.

Negotiating with Your Business Energy Provider

It's possible to negotiate a better deal from your energy company if you prepare and understand what you can negotiate on. Here are some tips to getting the best price for your energy bill:

Paragraph A
The more your energy provider knows about your current usage, the less likely they are to charge you a premium. Aim to give them at least 12 months of data showing your energy use for each half-hour period. This will show them your peak, shoulder and off-peak usage and your maximum demand, which may influence the network charges that you pay. You can obtain this data by contacting your energy provider.

Paragraph B
For smaller businesses on market retail contracts, ask your retailer about terms and conditions. Enquire about details on pricing and any discounts with an offer, such as pay on time discounts. If you negotiate your contract, review it before making any changes to your energy use or contract. While reviewing your contract, it's important to look for any special clauses. Some contracts include a 'take-or-pay' clause that means if you use less than a minimum amount of energy, you still have to pay. Contracts and clauses vary between energy retailers, so it may be worth doing some research or talking to an energy broker to discuss your options.

Paragraph C
You can easily do an online search to see how your energy contract compares to similar businesses. You can also consider using an energy broker or third party to get a better deal. When you're shopping around, make sure you bear in mind any broker or exit fees in your comparison. Search the Energy Made Easy website to compare electricity and gas offers.

Paragraph D
If you negotiate a contract, you don't have to wait until the end of your contract to begin a new one or get a better deal. Energy prices can change throughout the year, so consider negotiating on a low priced day or when the market prices are going down.

Paragraph E
The term of your energy contract is another way you can save money. By understanding the market, you can adjust your market contract period to suit. In a rising market, where current prices are cheaper than future prices, it may be better to choose a longer contract. In a decreasing market, it may be better to select a short period, with the aim of buying cheaper in the future.

Paragraph F
When negotiating your contract, it's important to consider any major developments you plan for your business. If you plan to expand your operations, consider a shorter contract until you have a better idea of the energy you'll need.

SECTION 3   Questions 28 – 40

Read the following passage and answer Questions **28 – 40**.

A Short History of the Passport

Paragraph A
The first reference to a document enabling passengers to travel across borders is when the Persian king Artaxerxes gave a letter "to governors of the province beyond the river" asking them to offer court official, Nehemiah, safe passage. This kind of letter is also mentioned in Shakespeare's *Henry V*, when the king, before Agincourt, declares: "He which hath no stomach for this fight, let him depart; his passport shall be made." There is a minor linguistic debate about whether the term 'passport' is to do with ports. In medieval Europe, travellers were issued documents by local authorities, so they could pass through the porte (gate) of city walls. The counter theory is that many royal letters of request – literally called passe ports, because they allowed the bearer to travel from ports in ships – were signed by the French king, Louis XIV. England's letters of safe conduct were first written in Latin and English, but in 1772, the government decided to use the international language of high finance and diplomacy: French. This didn't change until 1858, which meant that Britain's passports were issued in French, even as the British fought Napoleon.

Paragraph B
In the nineteenth century, the passport system began to collapse as railways crisscrossed Europe, and the amount of bureaucracy of issuing such documents and checking those of every person travelling seemed pointless. In 1861, France abolished passports and many European countries happily followed suit. The passport returned, however, during the First World War in an effort to reduce espionage. As a result, Britain produced the first recognisably modern passport as a single page, folded into eight, with a cardboard cover, a photograph of the bearer and a note of such details as shape of face and features. Peace resumed in 1918, but the passport stayed and the passport format was internationally standardised in 1920.

Paragraph C
As passports became more standardised, officials also added markedly modern demands for applications. Applicants had to produce supporting documents to prove their identity. Forms demanded consistently spelled full names and dates of birth. The passports themselves began consistently listing objective physical features of the bearer, such as height and eye color, as well as the stark, square headshot photo. Designated government clerks now checked all of the information, all with the idea of creating a verifiable identity that couldn't be easily assumed or forged.

Paragraph D
Although passports are important for the citizens of every country, the utility of some passports can be seen as greater than others. One method to measure the 'value' of a passport is to calculate its 'visa-free score,' which is the number of countries that allow the holder of that passport entry for general tourism without requiring a visa. Germany scores highest with this criterion, as their passport holders can travel without a visa to 161 countries. Sweden and Singapore come next with 160.

Questions 35 – 37

Choose the correct letter **A, B, C or D**. Write the correct letter in boxes **35 - 37** on your answer sheet.

35 Early British letters of safe conduct were often written in French, because

- **A** it made things easier in time of war.
- **B** it cost less for them to be written.
- **C** it was more acceptable for travellers at that time.
- **D** not enough people understood Latin.

36 Photographs were first used in passports, because

- **A** the British government did not consider only a physical description was enough.
- **B** it made it more difficult for enemies of Britain to travel.
- **C** so many people were travelling.
- **D** it created less bureaucracy dealing with other details.

37 Some countries' passports are perceived as being more valuable, because

- **A** no identity card is required.
- **B** they give people the right to live in more desirable countries.
- **C** travel within Europe is easier.
- **D** they require fewer visas to travel the world.

Questions 38 – 40

Complete each sentence with the correct ending (**A - F**) below. Write the correct letter (**A - F**) in boxes **38 - 40** on your answer sheet.

38 The ePassport gate is seen as particularly advantageous, because

39 The passport of the United States is viewed as particularly symbolic, because

40 The encrypted biometric passport's key was first broken, because

A the series of the information used was too obvious.

B fewer employees are required.

C it saves a lot of time.

D it is so hard to obtain.

E it can serve the same role as an identity card.

F an employee was bribed with two hundred dollars.

WRITING

WRITING TASK 1

You should spend about 20 minutes on this task.

> **You borrowed something recently from one of your friends, but unfortunately, you damaged it.**
>
> **Write a letter to your friend. In your letter,**
>
> - **explain what it is you borrowed and when you borrowed it**
> - **describe the damage and how it happened**
> - **explain what you intend to do about it**

You should write at least 150 words.

You do **NOT** need to write any addresses. Begin your letter as follows:

> *Dear John / Jane,*

WRITING TASK 2

You should spend about 40 minutes on this task.

Write about the following topic:

> **Many schoolchildren today take part in work experience sessions for short periods of time instead of attending school.**
>
> **Is this a positive or a negative development?**

Give reasons for your answer and include any relevant examples from your knowledge or experience.

You should write at least 250 words.

SPEAKING

PART 1

- Can you tell me about something you were good at when you were younger?
- Do you still do this thing? / Would you like to still do this thing? (Why?/Why not?)
- Is there anything you'd like to learn to do when you get older? (Why?/Why not?)

Topic 1   Driving and Cars

- Do you like driving a car? (Why?/Why not?)
- Do people drive well in your country? (Why?/Why not?)
- Do you think the world will change to electric cars soon? (Why?/Why not?)
- Do you think cars should be banned from city centres? (Why?/Why not?)

Topic 2   Crime

- What would you do if you saw a crime being committed?
- Do you think all guns should be illegal for the public? (Why?/Why not?)
- Do you think that there will be more or less crime in the future? (Why?/Why not?)
- Do you think that some illegal drugs should be legalised? (Why?/Why not?)

PART 2

Describe a memorable photograph that you have seen.
You should say:
    who or what is in the photo
    where and when the photo was taken
    what is happening in the photo
and explain why this photo is so memorable.

PART 3

Topic 1   Memories

- What are some of your earliest memories?
- What can older people do to keep their memories sharp?
- What do you do to remember important information, such as for an exam?
- Do you agree with the statement that 'people who forget the past will repeat it'? (Why?/Why not?)

Topic 2   Childhood

- What dreams for the future did you have when you were a child?
- How have you changed since you were a child?
- How is it different being a child in your country today in comparison to 50 years ago?
- What are some of the school challenges today for children?

TEST 23   LISTENING

PRACTICE TEST 23

LISTENING

 Download audio recordings for the test here:
https://www.ielts-blog.com/ielts-practice-tests-downloads/

SECTION 1   Questions 1 – 10

Questions 1 – 5

Complete the form below.

Write **NO MORE THAN THREE WORDS AND/OR A NUMBER** *from the listening for each answer.*

Group 8 Security - New Employee Details	
Employee's Full Name	Louisa Jennifer (**1**) _____
Employee's Address	45 Sherborne Road Greenham
Employee's Postcode	(**2**) _____ 7HY
Employee's Home Telephone	01483 759 742
Employee's Cell Telephone	07854 (**3**) _____ 986
Employee's Grade Entry	Grade (**4**) _____
Employee's Section	Home Security (on the (**5**) _____ floor)

Questions 6 – 10

Complete the notes below.

Write **NO MORE THAN THREE WORDS** from the listening for each answer.

First Day at Group 8 Security

- Arrive at 8 a.m.
- Find Anna and get my (**6**) _____ (she'll know I'm coming).
- I don't need to bring a photo.
- After Anna, go to meet department head (4th floor) quick tour of department + whole building.
- At 10 a.m., go to 8th floor meeting room for a 2-hour long orientation.
- Bring my (**7**) _____ + bank details. I'll get my computer + copier passwords.
- I will need to sign some paperwork.
- There are drinks stations on all floors with free tea, coffee, water and juices. (**8**) _____ available to eat there as well.
- There's a basement canteen with good, cheap (as they're subsidised) meals available.
- After lunch, return to my department and see my work space and probably my first (**9**) _____.
- Generally, people start work between 7 a.m. and 10 a.m. and finish between 4 p.m. and 7 p.m.
- Lunch can be taken between 11 a.m. and 3 p.m.
- I have to do an 8-hour day.
- No need to sign in or out - I (**10**) _____ my ID every time I go in or out of the building.

SECTION 2   Questions 11 – 20

Questions 11 – 15

Answer the questions below.

Write **NO MORE THAN TWO WORDS** from the listening for each answer.

11   What part of the natural equilibrium of nature would be affected if the gorilla became extinct?

12   What aspect of the gorillas' habitat does Linda say causes the habitat to be so cold?

13   What is the part of the mountain gorillas' diet that is so rich in water?

14   For what reason do people usually destroy mountain gorilla habitat?

15   What do local people use as a heat source in the areas where mountain gorillas live?

Questions 16 – 20

Match the gorilla (questions **16 - 20**) with the behaviour (**A - G**).

Choose **FIVE** letters from the box below, **A - G**, and write them on the answer sheet.

16   Simba

17   Linda

18   Jojo

19   Leila

20   Tommo

Behaviour
A   This gorilla is good with cameras.
B   This gorilla is sick.
C   This gorilla is very lively.
D   This gorilla is usually asleep during the day.
E   This gorilla is shy.
F   This gorilla is very caring.
G   This gorilla hasn't been seen for a while.

SECTION 3 Questions 21 – 30

Questions 21 – 25

Choose the correct letter **A, B or C**.

Write the correct letter in boxes **21 - 25** on your answer sheet.

21 What does Chris suggest that they do after 3 hours of driving?

  A Stop for a break
  B Drive through the rush hour
  C Change drivers

22 Who will share the driving for the trip to Conway?

  A Lizzie, Chris and Jennifer
  B Chris and Jennifer
  C Lizzie and Chris

23 What's the total cost of the minibus?

  A 450 pounds
  B 408 pounds
  C 350 pounds

24 Which day will the group **NOT** be researching near the sea?

  A Monday
  B Tuesday
  C Wednesday

25 What will the group do for lunch on Wednesday?

  A The hostel will give them a lunch to take with them
  B They will get lunch from a shop
  C The guide will bring their lunch

Questions 26 and 27

Match the student (questions **26 and 27**) with the room they will stay in (**A - F**).

Choose **TWO** letters from the plan below, **A - F**, and write them on the answer sheet.

26 Angela

27 Sebastian

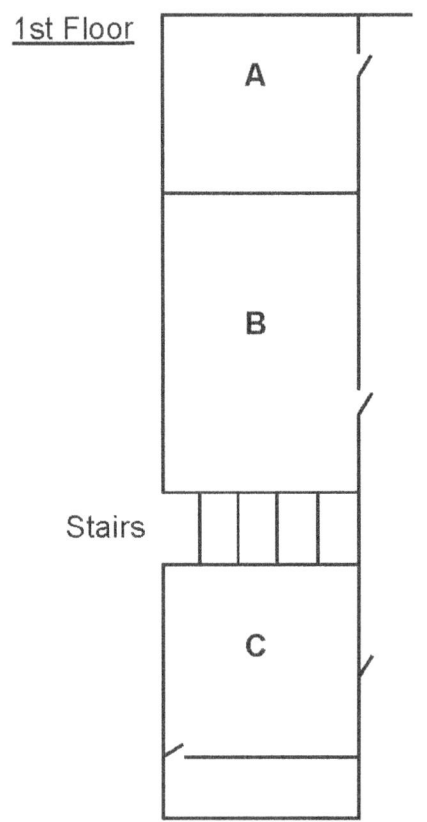
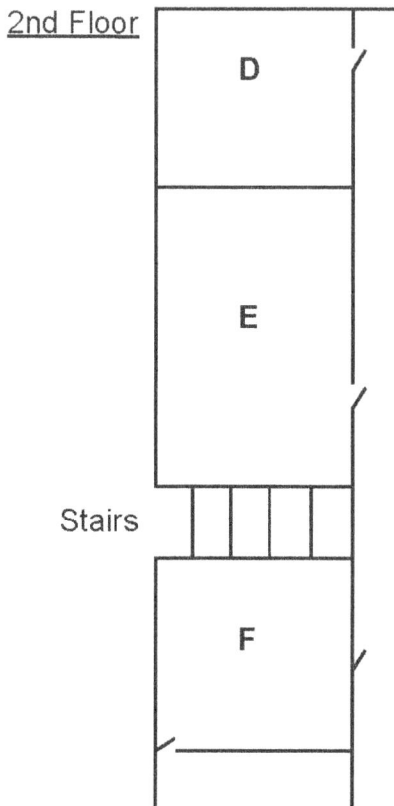

Questions 28 – 30

Answer the questions below.

Write **NO MORE THAN TWO WORDS** from the listening for each answer.

28 What doesn't work properly on the floor where the girls are staying?

29 What signal is given at the hostel to warn the students that meals will be starting?

30 What must the students give to the hostel when they receive their room keys?

SECTION 4   Questions 31 – 40

Questions 31 – 34

Choose the correct letter **A, B or C**.

Write the correct letter in boxes **31 - 34** on your answer sheet.

31   What technological advance made solar powered model aircraft possible in the 1970's?

    A   Smaller sized batteries
    B   Cheaper batteries
    C   Lighter batteries

32   Why did the Solar Challenger land during its initial flight?

    A   Maintenance
    B   The weather
    C   A dead battery

33   For what is the Berblinger Prize given?

    A   Innovative aircraft design ideas
    B   Non fossil fuel aircraft design ideas
    C   Solar powered plane design ideas

34   Why was Helios destroyed?

    A   It went too high
    B   It hit birds
    C   Unexpected air movement

Questions 35 - 38

Complete the notes below.

Write **NO MORE THAN THREE WORDS** from the listening for each answer.

The Solar Impulse

The first Solar Impulse plane was the HBSIA. Its wingspan is the same as an Airbus A340 and its weight is similar to an (**35**) _____. Its physical and aerodynamic features make it wholly innovative.

The Solar Impulse HBSIA's 200m² of photovoltaic cells allow the motors to achieve 8 horsepower or 6 kilowatts (the same the Wright brothers had). 12,000 approx. photovoltaic cells made of 145 microns of monocrystalline silicon give lightness and efficiency - could be more efficient, but it would be too heavy.

The main design (**36**) _____ is the weight of the batteries and so a high aspect ratio wing with a (**37**) _____ is needed to give good aerodynamic performance. Four under-wing pods contain an electric motor, a lithium battery, and a charge and temperature management system. (**38**) _____ retains battery heat, so they function at the 8500m temperature (-40 °C). The motors' maximum power output is 10HP.

Questions 39 and 40

Label the diagram below.

Write **NO MORE THAN THREE WORDS** from the listening for each answer.

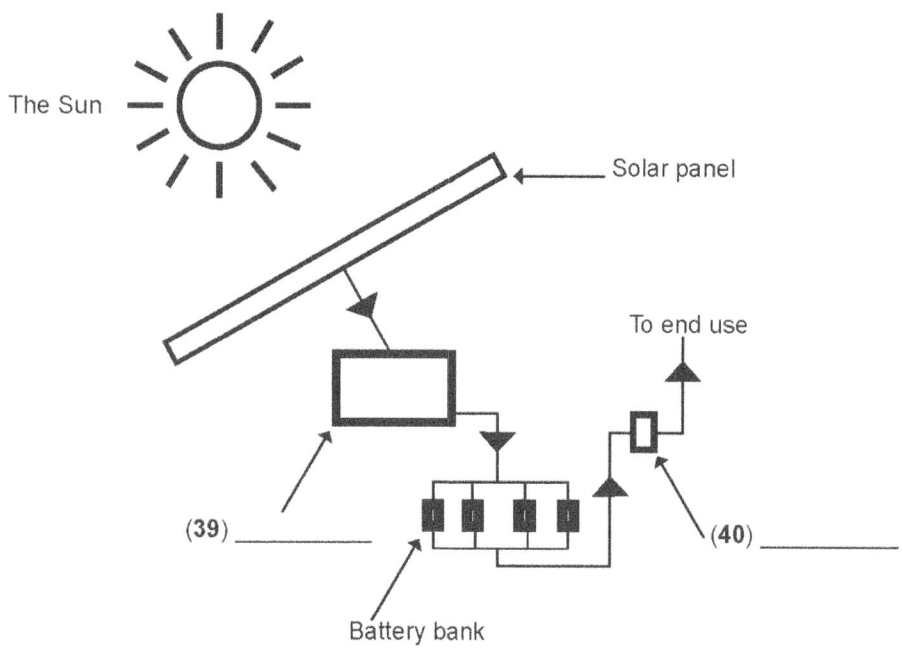

READING

SECTION 1   Questions 1 – 14

Questions 1 – 6

Answer the questions below.

Write **NO MORE THAN THREE WORDS** from the text for each answer.

Write your answers in boxes **1 - 6** on your answer sheet.

1. What will provide travellers shopping information at Petersfield Airport?

2. What can travellers do to be sure of being admitted to the Petersfield Airport lounge?

3. What free bonus can travellers enjoy if they buy a meal at one of the airport's food outlets?

4. What can travellers use while eating to find out about the status of their flight?

5. How can travellers access the Internet if they have no device of their own?

6. What is required to be shown to use the currency buy back service at Petersfield Airport?

Welcome to Petersfield Airport

Welcome to our airport! Whether you're departing or arriving, we hope that our facilities allow you to have an enjoyable and stress-free journey.

Petersfield Airport presents shopping access to the best of local and international brands, offering you an exceptional shopping experience. If you don't want to just browse, take advantage of the interactive consoles that will give you details of all our stores. Make sure that you check-in early and allow plenty of time to enjoy great shopping and the fantastic savings available!

Travelling can be a tiring process and arriving at your destination with a stiff body is a common experience. Why not spend your time lifting weights, working out, using the elliptical trainer or treadmill, or even taking a spin class and losing weight while waiting for your flight? Access to our state-of-the-art gym is $20 for an hour – power showers and luxury towels inclusive.

Petersfield Airport has elegant, modern and fully equipped guest rooms, so that you can sleep or rest comfortably for a few hours while waiting for your flight departure time. This service is ideal for passengers in transit, passengers who want to sleep the night before their flight at the airport, or passengers arriving at the airport well in advance of the departure of their flight.

Once you've left security behind you, you can leave the noise, crowds and chaos behind too. Our private lounge transforms the airport experience into a moment of indulgence. For a flat fee of $25, you get better WiFi, complementary newspapers, snack food and drinks, and sports and entertainment television. Lounge access is always subject to availability, so it's advised to book online to ensure you're not disappointed.

Petersfield Airport offers two different eating options: the à la carte restaurant and a self-service area. Take advantage of the salad bars (available on the house with a purchased main meal) at both restaurants. In all eating areas, you will have view of departure boards, giving you up-to-date information on your flight.

Need to be online while you're on the move? You can work, browse and keep in touch via wireless broadband or using Internet-connected PC's. There's Wi-Fi available throughout the terminal to help you stay in touch or plan your travels. Just choose 'Petersfield Wi-Fi' and follow the on-screen instructions. Once registered, you'll receive free Wi-Fi for the duration of your stay at Petersfield Airport.

There are frequent and regular direct bus and direct train services from the centre of Petersfield. Tickets can be bought in advance online, at the stations or on the bus or train. Road infrastructure around the airport is excellent and there are reasonably priced short-, medium- and long-term car parks.

Petersfield Airport has money-changing services that will ensure that you get the most competitive rates, convenience and value for money. We offer over 70 currencies and are open every day that the airport is open. It's hard to know how much currency you are going to need when abroad. Because of this, our money changing kiosk in Arrivals will buy back your leftover bank notes commission free at the original exchange rate that you paid. Please have the receipt if you wish to take advantage of this service. Receipts can be sent by email for your convenience and safety.

Questions 7 – 11

Complete the sentences below.

Write **NO MORE THAN TWO WORDS** from the text for each answer.

Write your answers in boxes **7 - 11** on your answer sheet.

7   The _____ of tickets stops when visitors exit the zoo.

8   Only the zoo's _____ may be used to feed the zoo's animals.

9   Parents must take note of and follow the _____ relating to any play areas.

10   People can often find things they have lost at the _____.

11   _____ is needed from the zoo if people wish to take any pictures for commercial purposes.

Visiting the Town Zoo

We would like you to remember your visit to our town's Zoological Gardens as an unforgettable and happy experience. Please show regard for the other visitors and the special needs of the animals. This means that you should assume responsibility for your own behaviour and be polite towards other visitors.

1. Tickets   You may only enter the Zoo with a valid ticket at the designated entrances. Please keep your ticket handy when entering the Zoo, so that you can show it to staff upon request. When you leave the Zoological Gardens, your ticket's validity will expire.

2. Parking   The Zoo's car park belongs to our grounds and it may only be used by visitors to the Zoological Gardens. Its use is regulated by the road traffic regulations and the displayed parking rules. The use of the car park is subject to a fee.

3. Feeding and Petting   Although animals may often appear to be tame and may win our affection when begging for food, their welfare and health can only be ensured when they are exclusively fed using the fodder of the zoo. We would therefore like to request that you do not attempt to feed the animals. At compounds where the Zoo offers you the opportunity to feed the animals, please only give the animals what has been provided by the Zoo.

4. Security Barriers   Please do not step outside the visitor's walkways and the specifically designated visitors areas. Also please keep off the grass and the flowerbeds. We would furthermore like to urgently advise you not to climb onto or over the security barriers or fences.

5. Pets Prohibited   Out of consideration for our animals and other visitors, pets (dogs, cats, etc.) are strictly prohibited in the Zoo. Guide dogs for the blind are welcomed.

6. Use of the Play Equipment   There are various play areas for children. Parents must be aware of the age restrictions, which must be strictly observed when using the play equipment, the playgrounds of the petting zoo and similar facilities.

7. Parental Responsibility   Children under the age of 12 may only visit the Zoological Gardens when accompanied by an adult. We would like to ask parents and people accompanying children and school groups to fulfil their supervision duty. Parents and persons accompanying children are liable for any damages caused by the persons under their supervision.

8. Reports on Damages and Loss of Items   The facilities of the Zoo are carefully maintained and monitored. Should you, however, sustain damage or a loss through no fault of your own, we would like to request that you report the event at the reception before leaving the Zoo. Lost and found items must also be handed in to the Zoo staff at the reception, where they can be picked up.

9. Photographing and Filming   Please feel free to take as many pictures and videos for your family memories as you would like. We would only like to ask that you respect the rights of the other visitors, as not everyone would like to have their picture taken. Please appreciate that the publication of photographs or film segments from the Zoo as well as photographs or films taken to make money require our approval.

Questions 12 – 14

Do the following statements agree with the information given in the text?

*In boxes **12 – 14** on your answer sheet write:*

TRUE *if the statement agrees with the information*
FALSE *if the statement contradicts the information*
NOT GIVEN *if there is no information on this*

12 Passengers leaving the temporary stops at Parkstone Playing Fields will experience slightly longer journeys.

13 The changes to bus routes and stops due to the pedestrianisation scheme will definitely not change for one year.

14 The town festival night buses will be free of charge.

Bus Route and Bus Stop Changes

The main bus station in Eddison Road will be undergoing renovations for one month from the start of June. All services starting from the Eddison Road bus station will now start at a line of temporary bus stops next to the Parkstone Playing Fields. Unfortunately, there will be no covered waiting area at this location. This temporary change will lead to all services arriving 4 minutes later than their usual scheduled time.

Your Council has been working on a pilot scheme to pedestrianise the High Street between Park Street and Katharine Hill. Various bus routes and stops have therefore been affected. These new arrangements are initially for approximately one year and are subject to alteration for operational reasons. We are working hard to keep the changes to a minimum. Your Council will review the impact of these changes, before either making them permanent, or returning to the previous arrangement next autumn. For more details on the pedestrianisation scheme please see the Council website.

The town festival will take place on the night of Saturday July 8th. All town night bus services will run later that night until 4 a.m. in order to help people get home safely and cheaply.

SECTION 2   Questions 15 – 27

Questions 15 – 21

Do the following statements agree with the views of the writer of the text?

In boxes **15 – 21** on your answer sheet write:

   YES   if the statement agrees with the writer's views
   NO   if the statement doesn't agree the writer's views
   NOT GIVEN   if it is impossible to say what the writer thinks about this

15   The most significant financial advantage of company cars for companies is the increase in sales' generation.

16   If the employee actually buys the car, he or she can set off the interest payments of a car loan against tax.

17   Companies must declare that an employee uses his/her company car for the employee's own purposes so that this benefit can be taxed.

18   Car insurance for companies is often cheaper.

19   Cars should usually be leased only as a perk for top management.

20   Receipts for claiming expenses back against tax have to be kept for 7 years after the relevant tax year.

21   The inclusion of a company car in a contract can help companies secure the best staff.

Company Cars

A car purchased for use in a business has certain tax advantages for the owner, whether that owner is the business or an employee. However, there are tax and other factors to consider in the decision to allow an employee to have a company car.

The biggest monetary benefit to the company from owning a business car is the cost savings from tax deductions. This deduction comes in two parts: the deduction for ownership of the car, and deductions for costs of driving the car for business purposes. For the business owner, the cost of the car as a business asset and the costs for business use of the car are both fully deductible from business taxes. For the employee, the cost of the car as an asset is not deductible (even for interest expenses on borrowing money to buy the car).

Specific Benefits of Business Ownership of a Company Car

- The company can deduct depreciation expenses at the rate in effect at the time the asset is put into service.
- The company can also deduct general auto expenses for business use of the vehicle, like maintenance, gasoline, and tyres.
- If the business owns the car, personal use of the car by the employee must be documented and the company must report personal use as taxable compensation.
- Interest on a car loan is deductible to a business as an ordinary and necessary business expense.
- Insurance for a company-owned car will probably be cheaper than for an employee-owned vehicle, since businesses can get leased-car and multiple-car rates and other discounts.
- If a company-owned car is involved in an accident, the driver's personal insurance rates and liability are minimised.

Many of the same issues are relevant if a business decides to lease a car for employee business use. Remember, however, that if you lease a car for an employee, you don't have much control over how much mileage the employee puts on that car. Many car lease terms have mileage restrictions and you may not be able to control personal use and keep costs down. Every situation is different, but it's nearly always the case that leased cars should be privileges for owners and executives; it's better to buy a car if an employee will be driving it.

Many expenses related to company cars can be deducted from corporation tax, but to be able to deduct these expenses, businesses must be able to provide proof. Business car expenses, like other business expenses, must be
- complete, showing all information including the date, location, mileage, and purpose.
- accurate, meaning you should have backups for individual expenses.
- timely, at the time of the expense, not created later.

Your employees must also be aware that they must separate business and personal use of the company car, whether it is their personal car or a business-owned car. Personal expenses are never deductible.

After you remove the taxation implication, it's difficult to put monetary costs on the financial value of a company car programme. The visibility, control and ability to deliver that such schemes provide can be invaluable. Aside from the significant benefits for recruitment and retention, the value of a company car programme to an organisation is only truly understood when it is not there or something goes wrong.

Questions 22 – 27

There is some advice on managing employee performance, **A – F,** on the next page.

Which section of the advice mentions the following information?

Write the correct letter, **A - F**, in boxes **22 - 27** on your answer sheet.

22   Clear notes should be kept of any meeting with an underperforming employee.

23   Behaviour that threatens the physical well-being of a fellow employee is not underperformance.

24   Performance management can help companies match their industry's competitors.

25   Better performance should be recognised.

26   Setting clear expectations at a meeting can help avoid accusations of victimisation at a later date.

27   Preventing underperformance is better than dealing with the consequences.

Managing Performance

Paragraph A
The best businesses are always improving their operations to stay competitive in their sector. To be able to do this, employees and managers need to be performing to a high standard. High performance in business means increased productivity, engaged and committed employees and retaining good employees. Poorly performing employees can have a negative effect on a business, for example they might create unhappy customers or clients, decrease productivity and create an unmotivated and underperforming workforce.

Paragraph B
Underperformance, or poor performance, is when an employee isn't doing their job properly, or is behaving in an unacceptable way at work. It includes various unacceptable behaviours and these behaviours should be recorded in the employee behaviour policy.

Paragraph C
It's important to understand the difference between underperformance and serious misconduct. The latter is when an employee causes serious and imminent risk to the health and safety of another person or to the reputation or profits of their employer's business, or deliberately behaves in a way that's inconsistent with continuing their employment. Examples of serious misconduct include theft, fraud, assault and refusing to carry out work duties.

Paragraph D
The best way to manage underperformance is to make sure it doesn't happen in the first place. Communication is the key. Steps that employers can take to help prevent underperformance include listing behavioural and outcome expectations in position descriptions, addressing any issues as soon as possible, having regular performance reviews to outline expectations from the beginning and encouraging employees to talk to a manager or employer if they have any questions or concerns.

Paragraph E
If an employee is underperforming, a private consultation can be arranged for the employee and employer to discuss the situation. It's a good idea for the employer to tell the employee what the discussion is about and ask them if they want to bring a support person along. Be clear about what the issues or concerns are and listen to the other person. Make sure both parties have discussed and agreed on a solution together, including clear and reasonable steps for improvement and document the meeting and outcomes. It's important to be clear about what could happen and what the employee's responsibilities are. This can also help prevent employees feeling they're being picked on if an issue does come up.

Paragraph F
After an employer has explained their concerns to an employee and provided them with strategies on how to improve performance, regular follow up meetings should be held. They can be used as an opportunity to talk about progress and see if there's any further help or support the employee needs, such as formal or informal training. Where performance has improved, employers should make sure they appreciate this.

SECTION 3   Questions 28 – 40

Read the following passage and answer Questions 28 – 40.

The Story of Vanilla

Vanilla is a member of the orchid family, a sprawling conglomeration of some 25,000 different species. Vanilla is a native of South and Central America and the Caribbean and the first people to have cultivated it seem to have been the Totonacs of Mexico's east coast. The flavour and fragrance of vanilla varies according to where it is grown and there are four main Vanilla-producing regions: Madagascar, Indonesia, Mexico and Tahiti.

Vanilla grows as a clinging vine, reaching lengths of up to 300 feet, from which sprout pale greenish-yellow flowers, about four inches in diameter. Vanilla in its native habitat is pollinated by bees. Each flower remains open for just 24 hours, after which, if not pollinated, it wilts, dies, and drops to the ground. In terms of farming it, this means that vanilla flowers need to be hand-pollinated.

The problem with vanilla is that it costs a lot. It is the second most expensive spice in the world (after saffron), because its production is so labour-intensive. "Vanilla requires a fair amount of skill to grow," explains Tom McCullum, co-founder of a direct-trade chocolate and vanilla company. "You can't just put seed in the ground, tend to it and expect it to produce a yield. Hand pollination is a learned skill. Many farmers have been growing vanilla for three to four generations. Smallholder farmers have an absolute sixth sense as to when the orchids will bloom."

Once pollination is completed, in approximately nine months, a fully-grown green bean is ready to be picked. The characteristic vanilla aromas and flavours don't reveal themselves until the crop is cured and dried, so it's also important to know how to manage the beans once they're harvested. Farmer Alex Ellis explains. "Vanilla beans are sorted and graded. They are then blanched in hot water to halt fermentation and placed in large containers to sweat for 36 to 48 hours. It's at this stage, when the beans start to change from green to brown, that they start to develop aroma." From there, the beans undergo alternating periods of sun drying during the day and sweating at night, a process that ends with a period of slow drying. "This usually occurs indoors, in a well-ventilated room where beans are placed on racks," Ellis says. "It can take up to 30 days, depending on the grade." The entire process, from growing to preparing for export, takes around one year.

Vanilla is a stunningly complex and subtle spice, containing somewhere between 250 and 500 different flavour and fragrance components. Botanist Sylvia Karner explains that these wonderful attributes have created a different industry. "The most prominent of the components is vanillin, which can be artificially made from petrochemicals and from eugenol, a component of clove oil. As total worldwide vanilla production is only about 2000 metric tons, this does not satisfy demand. Therefore the vast bulk of vanilla-flavoured products on the market don't actually contain vanilla. 98 per cent of the world's vanilla consumption is artificial and only 2 per cent is real. Products that are labelled as having vanilla essence in them contain this artificial vanillin."

Right now, this demand for inexpensive vanilla flavouring comes with an environmental cost. According to eco-farming lecturer Anna Winter, "the production of artificial vanillin creates a stream of wastewater that requires treatment before it can be released into surface water.

Catalysts currently used in the manufacturing of vanillin are also polluting and can only be used one time." Scientists are trying to develop a new catalyst that removes the polluting step, but without success so far. This catalyst could theoretically be re-used and, they hope, lead to more environmentally-friendly ways of manufacturing the alluring compound.

Vanilla production is also affected by changing world prices. "Vanilla's price volatility is historic," says Patricia Roberts, a dealer in vanilla. "In part, it is the result of cycles of tropical storms, something that may change in unpredictable ways due to climate change." Prices are also affected by how the vanilla bean matures. Vanilla beans start to ferment as soon as they are harvested, so there is an urgent need for farmers to find buyers for their beans. Smaller producers typically sell green beans to middlemen, who collect larger amounts of beans and sell them to centralised curing facilities, or directly to the curing facilities themselves. However, as there is no set market price for green beans, these farmers have limited options when it comes to negotiating for a higher price. "The money starts to pick up," Roberts says, "when it reaches those who cure and dry the beans. The vanilla then goes through many more sets of hands with prices going up each time." Those hands extend from traders who ship the beans to stores that stock them. "When prices for cured beans drop due to price speculation or an increased global supply," economist Salim Aziz explains, "farmers tear up crops. They can't afford to keep growing vanilla when prices stay so low." A decade ago, the prices for green beans dropped to 20 dollars a kilo and remained there for 5 years. The following price increase was built on speculation that, due to poor pollination, the vanilla crop would be small.

So how does all this affect the vanilla we buy in markets? Patricia Roberts says it's necessary to assess the vanilla bean before our purchase. "You should be able to take a bean, tie it around your finger, and untie it. That's how supple a good vanilla bean should be. Also, in terms of appearance, avoid extraordinarily large beans, as they were likely not cured properly."

Questions 28 – 35

Look at the following statements (questions 28 - 35) and the list of people below.

Match each statement with the correct person's initials.

Write the correct initials in boxes 28 - 35 on your answer sheet.

28   Some chemicals used in the production of vanillin cannot be recycled.

29   It is when vanilla beans change colour during treatment that they develop their important characteristics.

30   The quality of a vanilla pod can be assessed by its flexibility.

31   More vanilla is required than farmers can produce.

32   A lack of cash flow leads many farmers to stop growing vanilla.

33   Great skill and experience is required to know how to hand-pollinate the vanilla flower.

34   The quantities of vanilla produced is often subject to weather patterns.

35   Processing vanilla beans requires a location with good air circulation.

TM	Tom McCullum
AE	Alex Ellis
SK	Sylvia Karner
AW	Anna Winter
PR	Patricia Roberts
SA	Salim Aziz

Questions 36 – 38

Complete the flow chart below.

*Write **NO MORE THAN ONE WORD** from the text for each answer.*

*Write your answers in boxes **36 – 38** on your answer sheet.*

Producing Vanilla

Vanilla flowers for only 24 hours - hand pollination is needed if it's farmed, as the usual (**36**) _____ would not be reliable.

↓

Harvesting takes place 9 months following pollination.

↓

Following sorting and grading, blanching prevents (**37**) _____.

↓

Sweating for up to 2 days, followed by 5 days of alternate sweating and drying, allows the bean to develop correctly.

↓

Gradual (**38**) _____ ends the treatment process and the beans are exported.

Questions 39 and 40

*Choose the correct letter **A, B, C or D**.*

*Write the correct letter in boxes **39 and 40** on your answer sheet.*

39 Vanilla farmers must sell their beans to dealers quickly

    A   to keep sustainable cash flow.
    B   as the beans will otherwise go bad.
    C   because poor weather can ruin a crop.
    D   as beans need to be processed in large quantities to be commercially viable.

40 Worries about a recent poor vanilla harvest

    A   led to farmers destroying their crops.
    B   led to dealers storing crops from the previous year.
    C   led to a rise in prices.
    D   led to some farmers going out of business.

WRITING

WRITING TASK 1

You should spend about 20 minutes on this task.

You have recently noticed that your work computer is getting too slow and out-of -date.

Write a letter to your manager. In your letter,

- **explain the problems with your computer**
- **give some examples of how this has affected your work**
- **make some suggestions for what can be done to help address this issue**

You should write at least 150 words.

You do **NOT** need to write any addresses. Begin your letter as follows:

Dear Mr / Mrs Johnson,

WRITING TASK 2

You should spend about 40 minutes on this task.

Write about the following topic:

In some cities, the numbers of tourists seem to be overwhelming.

What are the effects of this on individuals and society?

Give reasons for your answer and include any relevant examples from your knowledge or experience.

You should write at least 250 words.

SPEAKING

PART 1

- What do you usually do in the evening?
- Is watching television a popular thing to do in the evening in your country? (Why?/Why not?)
- What time do you usually go to bed? (Why?)

Topic 1   Buses

- Do you like travelling by bus in your country? (Why?/Why not?)
- How can we persuade more people to take the bus rather than driving their own cars?
- Is public transport a reliable way to travel in your country?
- What do you do to pass the time on long journeys?

Topic 2   Water

- Do you drink a lot of water? (Why?/Why not?)
- Where does your town's water come from?
- Do you think access to water should be free? (Why?/Why not?)
- Do you ever worry about the availability of drinkable water? (Why?/Why not?)

PART 2

> Describe a memorable meal that you have eaten.
> You should say:
>   what you ate during the meal
>   where you ate the meal
>   who you ate the meal with
> and explain why this meal was so memorable.

PART 3

Topic 1   Vegetarianism

- Do you think that vegetarianism is healthy? (Why?/Why not?)
- Could you be a vegetarian for a day, a month or for ever? (Why?/Why not?)
- What are some of difficulties that vegetarians face?
- Do you think vegetarian parents should be allowed to make their children be vegetarians? (Why?/Why not?)

Topic 2   Food

- In what ways can today's food choices be considered unhealthy?
- What do you think about canned, frozen and processed food?
- Do you believe food advertising in your country is ethical? (Why?/Why not?)
- How has the food industry changed in your country over the last 50 years?

PRACTICE TEST 24

LISTENING

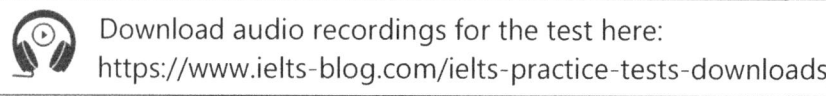

SECTION 1   Questions 1 – 10

Questions 1 – 5

Complete the sentences below.

Write **NO MORE THAN THREE WORDS AND/OR A NUMBER** from the listening for each answer.

1. The new family wishes to enrol with the Albans Dental Practice and they also want to sign up for the _____ package. *dental insurance*

2. Amelia Wood is _____ years old. *12*

3. The Wood's previous dental practice will send their dental records by *email*.

4. The Woods are waiting for the results of their *offer* on a nearby house.

5. Margaret Wood's husband's mobile telephone number is 07763 854 *118*.

Questions 6 – 10

Complete the table below.

*Write **NO MORE THAN TWO WORDS** from the listening for each answer.*

Dental Insurance Plan	Notes	Costs (All based on (10) _monthly payments_)
Core	<u>Fully Paid</u> • (6) _Routine_ examinations, hygiene treatments, gum disease treatments + dental x-rays <u>50% Paid</u> • remedial or restorative treatments (e.g. fillings, crowns, bridges and dentures) <u>Other Benefits</u> • Mouth cancer covered (£12,000) for 18 months following (7) _diagnosis_. (Smokers included) • Dental overseas travel insurance (£5000 for up to 4 incidents) (Cleaning not covered)	£30 per person £100 per family
Premium	• Same as the core plan, but cleaning is covered • Overseas cover is increased to (8) _ten thousand_ pounds • Tooth straightening procedures (braces) are covered (braces help children (9) _bite_ properly, eat more comfortably and dental care is easier; treatment lasts from 18 months – 2 years)	£45 per person £150 per family

SECTION 2 Questions 11 – 20

Questions 11 – 15

Complete the summary below.

Write **NO MORE THAN THREE WORDS** from the listening for each answer.

The Yardley Exercise Club

The Yardley Exercise Club does 4 different exercise activities weekly from Monday to Thursday. A different designated (11) _planner_ organises each activity. A monthly party is held at a member's house; a small (12) _fee_ (modest) is paid by everyone to the host. To be part of the club, members should pay £10 by direct debit on the first of every month - the money is used for (13) _bookings_ and insurance. New members should ensure Jack Lane has their email addresses and mobile numbers for the weekly email and text message explaining the week ahead's plan (this can also be seen on the website. Activities always start at seven p.m., though in order to avoid (14) _injury_, people should arrive a little early for the warming-up exercises. Any injuries can be treated in a basic way by a trained member, who will also have the club's (15) _first-aid kit_ with him or her.

Questions 16 – 20

Complete the flow chart below.

Write **NO MORE THAN ONE WORD** from the listening for each answer.

Yardley Exercise Club - Weekly Activities

Mondays	Running	Albert

Either a 5- or 8-km run.
People don't get lost due to the (**16**) _routes_ followed.

↓

Tuesdays	Swimming	Alison

2 lanes (1 slow, 1 medium/fast) always booked at the Yardley Sports Club.
Members should bring (**17**) _goggles_ along with the usual swimming kit.

↓

Wednesdays	Cycling	Stan

Reasonably challenging routes planned with little (**18**) _traffic_.
Members can get a discount when hiring a bike at Yardley's Bikes.
This activity takes place at a cycling track in the (**19**) _stadium_.

↓

Thursdays	Weights and Circuit Training	Jo

Again at Yardley Sports Club.
Probably the hardest (**20**) _challenge_ of the weeks' activities.

TEST 24   LISTENING

SECTION 3   Questions 21 – 30

Questions 21 – 25

Choose **FIVE** letters (**A - H**) and write them in any order in boxes **21 - 25** on your answer sheet.

*According to the conversation between Jonathan and Professor Williams, pick **FIVE** things that Jonathan is complaining about regarding Dr. Forrest.*

A	Dr. Forrest does not allow students to use computers during his classes.
B	Dr. Forrest has unfairly punished some students.
C	Dr. Forrest is not punctual.
D	Dr. Forrest sometimes speaks inappropriately.
E	Dr. Forrest often calls in sick.
F	Dr. Forrest does not provide digital copies of relevant papers.
G	Dr. Forrest does not answer student emails.
H	Dr. Forrest can show annoyance with his students.

21   C, D, F, G, H
22
23
24
25

Questions 26 – 29

Complete the notes below.

Write **NO MORE THAN TWO WORDS** from the listening for each answer.

The Causes of Algal Blooms

Algal blooms are encouraged by (**26**) _nutrients_ entering the water (mainly phosphorus and nitrogen). They come from:
- runoff and erosion from fertilised agricultural areas.
- river bank and bed erosion.
- land clearing.
- discharge of (**27**) _sewage_.

When sediments release phosphates because the water is low in dissolved oxygen, algal blooms can occur.

Blooms can happen with low (**28**) _concentration_ of phosphorus and nitrogen, but are more likely when high.

Temperature

Blooms more likely in warmer and lighter months - optimum temperature: 25 degrees Celsius. Algal blooms are rare in (**29**) _____ during the winter, but algal blooms can occur all the time in tropical areas.

Question 30

Choose **ONE** letter (**A - G**) and write it in box **30** on your answer sheet.

Which **ONE** of the following in humans or animals is **NOT** mentioned as being adversely affected by the toxins and irritants found in algae?

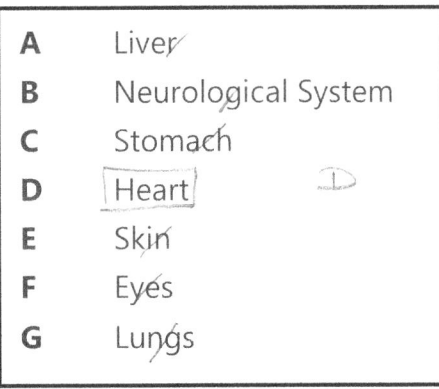

SECTION 4   Questions 31 – 40

Questions 31 – 33

Complete the summary below.

Write **NO MORE THAN ONE WORD** from the listening for each answer.

Recent Wind Power Exploitation

Wind projects have flourished since 1991, mostly in (**31**) _____ waters in Europe, but the U.S. is following. Improved (**32**) _____ will soon lead to wind projects in deeper water.

Wind has been exploited for millennia for different uses, but today, it's used mainly for producing electricity. Today's turbines all work in a similar way and the advanced engineering has improved (**33**) _____ and electrical generation.

Questions 34 – 37

Choose **FOUR** letters, **A - G**.

What **FOUR** from the following list are potential advantages to the U.S. wind energy industry?

A   The offshore winds around the U.S. blow quite reliably.

B   Sea-based projects are very popular with the general public.

C   The frequent U.S. low wind conditions actually produce surprisingly large quantities of electricity.

D   Not much new engineering is require to adapt land-based wind technology to sea-based projects.

E   Potential wind sites around the U.S. are not affected by ice in the sea.

F   Current sea-based wind turbines are well protected against rust.

G   Most potential wind sites around the U.S. are in shallow water.

Questions 38 – 40

Label the diagram below.

Write **NO MORE THAN THREE WORDS** from the listening for each answer.

An Offshore Wind Turbine

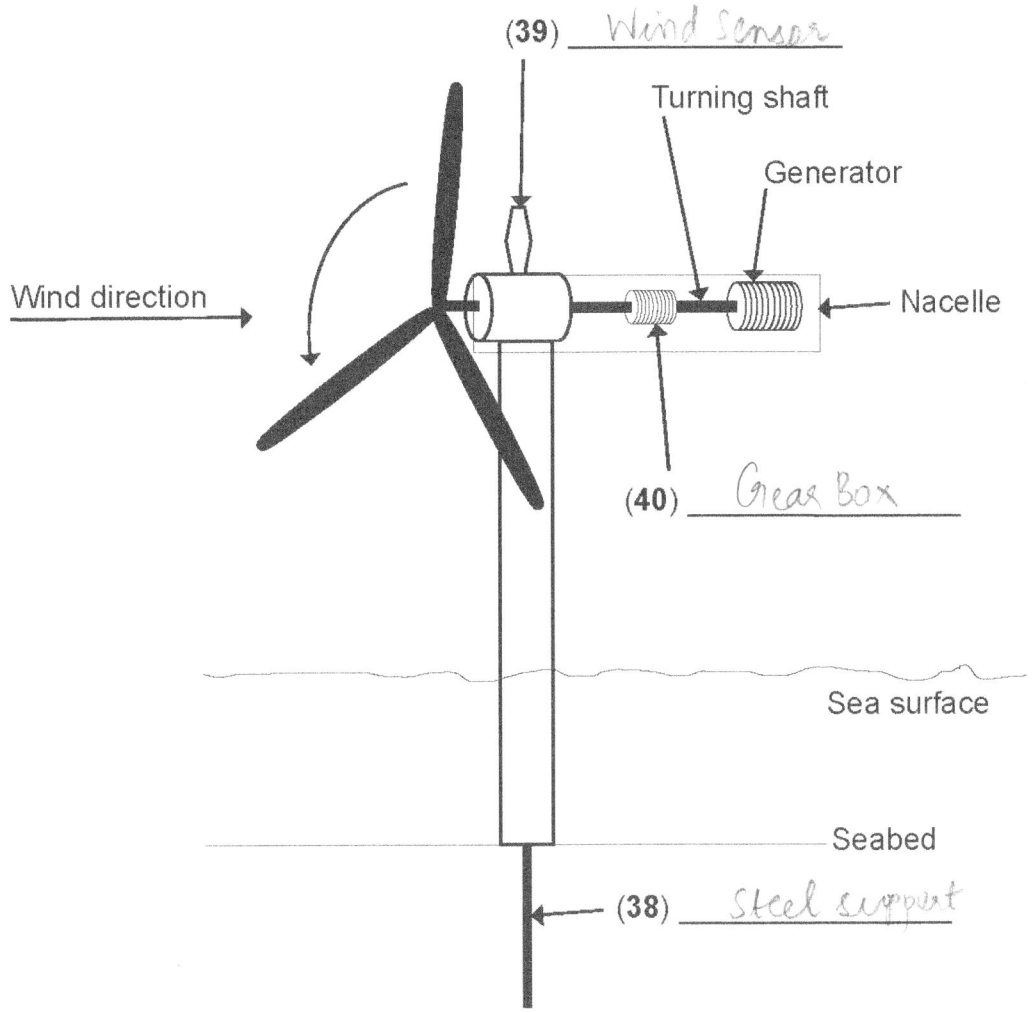

READING

SECTION 1   Questions 1 – 14

Questions 1 – 7

There are 5 advertisements **A – E** on the next page.

Answer the questions below by writing the letters of the appropriate advertisements in boxes **1 – 7** on your answer sheet.

1   Which advertisement states that its products can be bought on the Internet?

2   Which advertisement states that more than one destination can be visited?

3   Which advertisement states that mountains can be seen from the premises?

4   Which advertisement states that activities are available for children?

5   Which advertisement states that customers can be met in person?

6   Which advertisement states that how old customers are is not an issue?

7   Which advertisement states that laundry can be done?

A The Ocean View Hotel

With our wonderful en-suite rooms, award-winning restaurant, array of activity options and private beach, the Ocean View Hotel can provide you with your dream holiday. From a weekend away to a fortnight's break, let us provide you with a time away that will relax and rejuvenate you. We have 14 beautiful bedrooms, nine of which have sea views. The other three have panoramic views of the mountains that rise behind us. Check our website today to see the events and weekend specials that we'll be running over the next few months.

B Sandy Dune Camp Site

With the costs of hotel and guest house accommodation soaring, why not get away from it all in the great outdoors? Bring your own tent, or rent one of our tents or fixed cabins.

Hot showers, cooking and washing-up facilities, launderette, electric hook ups and TV connections are all standard at all our sites or pitches. Restaurant (take away or eat in) available for those who don't want to cook and wash up.

1 kilometre from the supervised sandy beach and safe sea-swimming. Indoor and outdoor play areas for children (supervised from 9 a.m. to 5 p.m., 7 days a week from start of July to end of August).

C Haileybury Transfers

We provide a licensed transfer service to and from any part of the country, 24 hours a day, 7 days a week. Our prices are very competitive and considerably lower than metered taxis at the taxi stands. Passengers can pre book their transfer service at fixed prices by calling us on 07629 873 672. We can also provide a meet and greet service at the airport, train or bus station and drive you to your destination in comfort. Please provide the essential data about your arrival when you make your booking and you will be picked up on your arrival by your friendly and professional driver with your name on a card.

D Atlas Travel Insurances

Wherever you're going on holiday, remember to pack travel insurance. Call us direct and speak to one of our representatives, or get instant cover online today.

From single trip to multi trip cover, we can provide everything your holiday may throw at you! No upper age limits!

E *Poseidon Holidays*

Do you want to wake up every morning in a new place? As a leading cruise specialist, we pride ourselves on our selection of cruises. From a vast choice of cruise lines and ships to a huge range of popular destinations around the world, our variety and impeccable service from the minute you book to the moment you arrive home make our cruise holidays unrivalled. We have a wide range of competitively-priced cruises, so you'll be sure to do the things you've always dreamed of at a time and date that suits you. Cruises are especially good for romantic getaways. From beautiful beaches and splash-tastic fun, to must-see sights and mouth-watering food – our range of couples cruise holidays has got just the destination for you and your beau. So grab your other half and get set for a show-stopping, eye-popping, whirlwind of a couple's cruise. They say that "food is the way to someone's heart", which is why our ships are jam-packed with places that serve up all-out delicious flavours at every meal. From Japanese delights to perfectly cooked steaks, you'll find something that both you and your other half will love.

Questions 8 – 14

Complete the sentences below.

Write **NO MORE THAN TWO WORDS** from the text for each answer.

Write your answers in boxes **8 - 14** on your answer sheet.

8 Use your door's _____ if you don't know who has rung the doorbell.

9 An _____ is a good alternative or addition to getting a dog.

10 _____ can be asked to monitor your house if you go away.

11 _____ is easier for burglars if your house and garden are not well lighted.

12 Watch what is put into the _____, as this can give burglars clues as to what you own.

13 A _____ can contact you if it detects movement at your property.

14 Having your _____ written on your property can help ensure your own property is returned if stolen.

Making Your Home More Secure Against Burglars

Home security is an important topic to address because many unpleasant things happen on a regular basis due to neglect from homeowners and renters.

Burglars and other intruders are a perennial threat. First there are the basic things – keep doors and windows locked, keep a light and radio on when you're away. Keep the chain on when answering the door and don't allow anyone into your home that you don't know. Keep in mind that any time you let someone into your home, you are giving them an opportunity to steal, scope out your valuables, and/or make plans to come back at another time to take your belongings that they have spotted.

Burglars don't like noise, so getting a dog is always a good way to scare them off. If getting a dog is not practical for you, then installing an alarm is a must. A home security camera is also a great thing to have, because it will keep tabs on people, and help you keep an eye on unwanted visitors and behaviour.

A great way to ward off unwanted visitors and potential burglars is to get friendly with neighbours, so that everyone can help each other out. This is especially helpful when/if you go on vacation for an extended period of time and need someone to help you keep a close eye on your property.

Thieves will frequent dark areas because it's easier for them to watch and conduct research for their burglaries and run away and not get caught. Having light around your home at night will keep your area well lit and more likely clear of criminals.

Some criminals will go through your trash to see what you've left behind. For example, if you recently bought an expensive TV and are throwing out the packaging, a criminal who sees that might use it as a clue and incentive to come back and find a way to get the TV. Make sure you cut up the packaging of your purchases and make it as inconspicuous as possible.

If you trim your bushes and eliminate potential hiding spots, thieves are a lot less likely to show up and try to steal from your home. Keeping your place well-kept also signifies that the home is lived in and that you're not away on vacation for an extended period of time.

Keeping your home safe is a lot easier now thanks to advanced technology. For example, remote monitoring cameras allow you to view activity in the home from work, vacation, or virtually anywhere outside of the home, on your phone. Even if you are miles away from home, you can still see in real-time what is going on. Many security systems nowadays also allow you to arm and disarm them remotely. This means that even if you forget to set the house security systems on before you leave, you can still do so from your phone. In addition to remote monitoring, smart locks also exist to automatically lock doors once they sense that you have left the home, using bluetooth on your phone. Another modern device is the motion sensor, which is great for detecting movement. When armed, it will turn on bright lights and send a message to your mobile device if it detects something. This way, you can be immediately notified if someone is trying to break into your house. Of course, the types of technology are endless, but these are a few common ones found in many homes.

If you do get burgled, make sure you have a list and photos of your valuables on hand and ready to report. Write your postcode on items like televisions in your house with an invisible ultraviolet ink pen. This will make your property easier to trace if it's found and it will also make your property harder to sell on.

SECTION 2   Questions 15 – 27

Questions 15 – 21

Complete the summary below.

Write **NO MORE THAN THREE WORDS** from the text for each answer.

Write your answers in boxes **15 - 21** on your answer sheet.

Cyber Security for Businesses

Good cyber security can protect various aspects of a business. A firewall can process all (**15**) _____ to see if it's safe to get within a business' network. A pre-installed personal firewall can be used or a bespoke system can be installed to create a (**16**) _____ between the business network and the Internet. Next, checking that the (**17**) _____ of new systems do not allow easy access to outsiders is something that needs to be done. All devices also need to be password-protected with appropriate passwords. Sensitive systems should use the added protection of the (**18**) _____ that is sent when using 2FA. A further necessary step is to use the (**19**) _____ that is again usually pre-installed on most systems. This protects against viruses and malware. Finally, staff (**20**) _____ should be restricted to what staff need. Staff with an (**21**) _____ should avoid surfing the web, as this can be riskier behaviour.

Cyber Security for Businesses

All organisations today should take basic steps to protect themselves online and you can take some simple steps to protect your business. Having good cyber security measures in place will help protect your cash flow, your customer data and your reputation.

The first thing you should do is to use a firewall to secure your Internet connection. This can analyse traffic to see if it should be allowed onto your network. There are two types of firewall. You could use a personal firewall on your Internet connected laptop (normally included within your Operating System at no extra charge). Or, if you have a more complicated set up with many different types of devices, you might require a dedicated system. The firewall effectively creates a buffer between your IT network and other, external networks, which in the simplest case means between your computer (or computers) and 'the Internet'. Some routers will contain a firewall that could be used in this role. Ask your Internet service provider about your specific model.

Another important thing to do is to choose the most secure settings for your devices and software. Manufacturers often set the default of new software and devices to be as open and multi-functional as possible. They come with 'everything on' to make them easily connectable and usable. Unfortunately, this can also provide cyber attackers with opportunities to gain unauthorised access to your data, often without difficulty. You should therefore always check new software and devices where possible and make changes which raise your level of security.

Your laptops, desktop computers, tablets and smartphones contain your data, but they also store the details of the online accounts that you access, so both your devices and your accounts should always be password-protected. Passwords, when implemented correctly, are an easy and effective way to prevent unauthorised users accessing your devices. Passwords should be easy to remember and hard for somebody else to guess. The preset user credentials that come with new devices such as 'admin' and 'password' are the easiest of all for attackers to guess. For 'important' accounts, such as banking and IT administration, you should use two-factor authentication, also known as 2FA. A common and effective example of this involves a code delivered to a smartphone that you must enter in addition to your password.

One thing that everyone knows about is how it's necessary to protect yourself from viruses and other malware, i.e. software or web content that has been designed to cause harm. There are various ways in which malware can find its way onto a computer. A user may open an infected email, browse a compromised website or open an unknown file from removable storage media, such as a USB memory stick. Antivirus software is often included for free within popular operating systems, so it should be used on all computers and laptops. For most office equipment, you can pretty much click 'enable', and you're instantly safer.

Finally, you need to control who has the right to view and edit data and services. To minimise the potential damage that could be done if an account is misused or stolen, staff should have just enough privileges to software, settings, online services and device connectivity functions for them to perform their role. Extra should only be given to those who need them, so check everyone's accounts. By ensuring as well that your staff don't browse the web from an administrative account, you cut down on the chance that it will be compromised. This is important because an attacker with unauthorised access to an administrative account can be far more damaging than one accessing a standard user account.

Questions 22 – 27

Complete the table below.

Write **NO MORE THAN THREE WORDS** from the text for each answer.

Write your answers in boxes **22 - 27** on your answer sheet.

Action	Notes
Perform credit checks on customers.	* This ensures customers pay on time.
Check that you can process orders, so that you don't overtrade.	* This ensures you have the production efficiency and enough good (**22**) _____ to process orders. * This overtrading can particularly threaten (**23**) _____. * Excessive (**24**) _____ are also very dangerous.
Check that you can take orders easily.	* Ensure sales can be placed in different ways. * (**25**) _____ should be clear and easy to use.
Use temporary actions to help.	* (**26**) _____ can help cover financial short falls – show potential (**27**) _____ your cash flow forecast to help get the money.

Cash Flow Management

Managing your cash flow is vital for business survival and growth. To run your business effectively, you need to balance the timing and amount of your costs with those of your income.

The business cliché 'cash is king' still rings true, and whether it is the result of under trading or over trading, getting the cash position wrong will not only destroy any hope of growth, but could also be the downfall of a small business. Firms that fall prey to cash flow problems often say they find it difficult to monitor and don't know how to rectify the situation when things are going wrong. However, if businesses can understand their cash position, then they can plan effective action, for example, modifying when they pay suppliers, chasing or encouraging customers to pay early, and cutting back on expenditure.

No matter how effective your negotiations with customers and suppliers, poor business practices can put your cash flow at risk. However, there are some practices you could introduce into your business to reduce the risk of cash flow problems. For example, you should think about running credit checks on your customers to ensure they can pay you on time. You also need to deliver on time. If you don't, or deliver to specification, you might not get paid. You should measure your production efficiency and the quantity and quality of the stock you hold and produce to ensure you can meet all your orders in a way that satisfies your customers.

It seems strange to worry about too many orders, but overtrading can be a danger for many businesses. Overtrading is an imbalance between the work that a business takes on and its capacity to do the work. This can happen when a business takes on work, but cannot live up to the resulting demands. This is particularly common in expanding businesses. It can be extremely serious, even fatal to an organisation, so it's worth taking time to understand how to prevent it happening to your business. Most businesses offer a maximum three-month period between product delivery and payment. The supplying businesses must of course continue to pay their own overheads and suppliers when due. If too many orders are taking up too much money, in order to pay, for example, for parts and labour, but the customers don't have to pay for a while, then companies can find their cash reserves dwindling very quickly. This is a very typical cash flow problem. Many cash flow problems also arise from too many overheads. In order to control these, you could consider outsourcing non-core activities, such as payroll services or review your utilities contracts to see whether it would be cheaper to switch tariff or supplier. Price comparison websites can help with this.

Another important factor that people don't consider enough is whether people can place orders with them easily. Check to see if you accept orders over the telephone, email or Internet, so that customers may be able to pay more quickly. You should also ensure order forms are clear and easy to use to improve the sales and payment processes. If you don't get the orders at all, then cash flow will of course dry up and your business will very quickly be in trouble.

Sometimes, after doing all you can, your cash flow forecast may still suggest potential cash flow problems. You should consider using something to help. Overdrafts for example can see you through temporarily. Having a cash flow forecast to demonstrate the shortfall is temporary will reassure finance providers. In order to do this, ensure that you keep up-to-date accounting records. This will also help warn you about taking orders you can't handle.

SECTION 3   Questions 28 – 40

Read the following passage and answer Questions **28 – 40**.

Men and women are equally affected by back pain, which can range in intensity from a dull, constant ache to a sudden, sharp sensation that leaves the person incapacitated. Pain can begin abruptly as a result of an accident or by lifting something heavy, or it can develop over time due to age-related changes of the spine. Sedentary lifestyles can also set the stage for back pain, especially when a weekday routine of getting too little exercise is punctuated by a strenuous weekend workout. Most back pain is acute and lasts from a few days to a few weeks, however, it can become chronic. It usually tends to resolve on its own with self-care and there is no residual loss of function. About 80 percent of adults experience back pain at some point in their lifetimes and it is the most common cause of job-related disability and sick days. In a large survey, more than a quarter of adults reported experiencing back pain during the previous three months.

Back pain is the leading cause of activity limitation and work absence throughout much of the world, imposing an extreme economic burden on individuals, families, communities, industry, and governments. Several studies have been performed in Europe to evaluate how back pain impacts society. In the United Kingdom, back pain was identified as the most common cause of disability in young adults, with more than 100 million workdays lost per year. In Sweden, a survey suggested that back pain accounted for a quadrupling of the number of work days lost from 7 million in 1980 to 28 million by 1987. However, the existence of social compensation systems in Sweden might account for some of this increase. In the United States, an estimated 149 million work days are lost every year because of back pain, with total costs estimated to be a hundred billion to two hundred billion dollars a year, of which two-thirds is due to lower productivity.

The socio-economic impacts of back pain are varied. The cost of the actual treatment for patients with back pain has a major economic impact worldwide. In the United States, patients with musculoskeletal conditions incur total annual medical care costs of approximately $240 billion, of which $77 billion is related to musculoskeletal conditions. Approximately 35 per cent of the financial expenses related to back pain are for services provided in the private sector and thus are most likely paid for directly by patients and their families. With respect to the distribution of the financial expenses across different providers, 37 per cent relate to care provided by physiotherapists and allied specialists, 31 per cent are incurred in the hospital sector, 14 per cent relate to primary care, 7 per cent to medication, 6 per cent to community care and 5 per cent to radiology and imaging used for investigation. However, the direct expenses of back pain are insignificant compared to the cost of informal care and the production losses related to it, which total billions of dollars in most countries.

Informal care is an area that impacts society significantly. Today in the UK, around one in fifty of adults over 35 is an unpaid carer, looking after a friend or family member with back pain. As well as the loss of their own work, unpaid carers are a group that creates loss of work due to the physical and psychological factors involved and they themselves often present to healthcare services as secondary patients. Unpaid carers actually save countries enormous amounts of money. Last year, the work of unpaid carers saved the UK National Health Service up to 119 billion pounds, though not all of these carers were involved with people with back pain.

Whatever the different impacts of back pain are, the estimates of the economic burden of chronic back pain do not do justice to the extent of suffering and decreased quality of life experienced by patients. It is not just the economic impact, but rather the tremendous human suffering resulting from chronic pain. Pain affects everyone to varying degrees. For some, it may be the briefest of acute sensations, but for others it becomes a permanent feature of their lives and its effects on well-being can be wide reaching, leading to depression, sleep disturbance and fatigue, decrements in physical and cognitive functioning, and changes in mood, personality, and social interactions of the sufferer. Thus, although the wider impacts of chronic back pain - in terms of suffering and impact on a person's life - are impossible to quantify with any degree of precision, it is clear that they come at a high price in terms of an individual's physical, psychological, and social well-being. Of course, on top of all this, society does pay the financial price of treatment and it also suffers the lost work of the sufferers and carers. Back pain is an affliction that has diverse socio-economic impacts at many different levels.

Questions 28 – 36

Complete the notes below.

*Write **NO MORE THAN THREE WORDS** for each answer.*

*Write your answers in boxes **28 - 36** on your answer sheet.*

- Back pain affects lots of people. It has different symptoms and different causes - inactive (**28**) _____ are a major contributor, in particular if hard exercise is suddenly but infrequently done.
- Usually, back pain is (**29**) _____, but it can also be long-term.
- Back pain is the most frequent reason for workplace incapacity and sick days.
- Back pain places a high financial (**30**) _____ on different areas of society and in different countries.
- The UK, Sweden and US lose a lot of work to back pain, with the latter losing significant money on (**31**) _____.
- Medical treatment expenses for back pain are significant – the sufferers and/or their (**32**) _____ pay for just over a third of this.
- Various treatment services are used – physiotherapy, specialists hospitals, care, drugs and scanning (the latter for (**33**) _____).
- Unpaid carers fulfil a vital societal role, though they too are affected because of physical problems they develop and (**34**) _____.
- There are various known impacts of back pain, but the pain and reduced (**35**) _____ is less well understood.
- Pain affects people in lots of different ways and has a variety of (**36**) _____ effects.

Questions 37 – 39

Choose the correct letter **A, B, C or D**.

Write the correct letter in boxes **37 - 39** on your answer sheet.

37   The work of UK unpaid carers

    A   is not sufficiently recognised by the government.
    B   shows that more training needs to be provided.
    C   prevents the government from having to spend money on carers.
    D   is not of sufficiently good standard.

38   Pain can affect people's psychological well-being, which can lead to

    A   unexpected changes in visual perception.
    B   people making more social contacts at treatment centres.
    C   overcrowding at hospitals.
    D   a deterioration in patients' social relationships.

39   The impacts of long-term back pain

    A   have been widely researched.
    B   cannot be accurately measured in figures.
    C   are worse for the male workforce.
    D   are not yet fully understood.

Question 40

Choose the correct letter, **A, B, C or D**.

Write the correct letter in box **40** on your answer sheet.

40   What is the best title for the text in section 3?

    A   What is Back Pain?
    B   Back Pain – An Affliction of Modern Society
    C   The Costs of Back Pain
    D   How to Treat Back Pain

WRITING

WRITING TASK 1

You should spend about 20 minutes on this task.

> **You recently had a meal in a restaurant in another town. Unfortunately, you left your mobile phone in the restaurant.**
>
> **Write a letter to the restaurant's manager. In your letter,**
>
> - **explain what happened**
> - **describe your mobile phone**
> - **make some suggestions about how you can get your mobile phone back**

You should write at least 150 words.

*You do **NOT** need to write any addresses. Begin your letter as follows:*

> *Dear Sir / Madam,*

WRITING TASK 2

You should spend about 40 minutes on this task.

Write about the following topic:

> **With the vast increase in online resources today, libraries with print books are not a necessity for today's society.**
>
> **To what extent do you agree or disagree with this statement?**

Give reasons for your answer and include any relevant examples from your knowledge or experience.

You should write at least 250 words.

SPEAKING

PART 1

- What can you see from one of the windows of your apartment or house?
- What do you have on the walls of your bedroom?
- Do you prefer a carpet or a wooden floor where you live? (Why?)

Topic 1   Challenges

- Do you like to challenge yourself? (Why?/Why not?)
- What are some of the day-to-day challenges that we face in the modern world?
- What can be the results of challenges that are too difficult?
- What are some of the challenges that will face the generations following us?

Topic 2   Forests

- Do you like walking in a forest? (Why?/Why not?)
- What are some of the dangers of being in a forest?
- What are some of the threats to forests?
- What can be done to preserve forests and other natural places?

PART 2

> Describe something memorable you've recently received in the post.
> You should say:
>
>   what this thing was
>   who sent it
>   what you do/did with it
>
> and explain why this thing is so memorable.

PART 3

Topic 1   The Postal Services

- What are the postal services like in your country?
- What are some of the advantages and disadvantages to communicating by the post rather than through modern media, such as email or text messaging?
- Do you think it's better for postal services to be in private or government hands? (Why?)
- How has your country's postal services reacted to today's volume of online shopping?

Topic 2   Communication

- What have been some of the most significant events in communication through history?
- What communication skills are particularly important in the 21st Century?
- How do you think communication will develop over the next 50 years?
- How important is body language in communication? (Why?)

PRACTICE TEST 25

LISTENING

 Download audio recordings for the test here:
https://www.ielts-blog.com/ielts-practice-tests-downloads/

SECTION 1   Questions 1 – 10

Questions 1 – 5

Complete the form below.

*Write **NO MORE THAN THREE WORDS AND/OR A NUMBER** from the listening for each answer.*

Netwave - Customer Service Form

Customer Account Number: (**1**) _____ 962Y

Customer Date of Birth: 16th (**2**) _____ 1975

Customer Postcode :   WH5 7JH

Customer Problem

Since Wednesday, the Internet connection became slower. Since (**3**) _____, there's been no connection at all. Probably a fault with the (**4**) _____. The customer will probably change over to our combined package.

Service Appointment

12th August at (**5**) _____ p.m.

Questions 6 – 10

Complete the summary below.

*Write **NO MORE THAN THREE WORDS AND/OR A NUMBER** from the listening for each answer.*

Netwave's Current Offers

Netwave will double our (**6**) _____ at no extra cost. I've agreed to this.

They can also combine our services of Internet, cable TV and telephone.
The current prices are:
    Internet $30 monthly
    Telephone Line Rental $10 monthly
    Cable TV $50 monthly

Netwave can combine these with their Homebase Package, which would cost $ (**7**) _____ monthly. We would have to extend our contract with Netwave to (**8**) _____ from now. If we're happy with this, the (**9**) _____ should have all the appropriate paperwork with her/him for us to sign.

We can now pay our Netwave bills by direct debit. I gave the customer services representative our bank details for this. Our reference number is: (**10**) _____.

SECTION 2 Questions 11 - 20

Questions 11 – 15

Complete the table below.

*Write **NO MORE THAN TWO WORDS AND/OR A NUMBER** from the listening for each answer.*

	Burley Bird Watching and Nature Club Information sheet
Club Information	The Club started in the year (**11**) _____. The Club meets on Wednesdays. The Club meets in the Burley Community Hall. The Club meets usually at 7.30 p.m. (usually meetings last for 3 hours approx.). The Club activities include socialising, discussion, guest speakers.
Fee Information	The Yearly Fee $80 The (**12**) _____ $60 (money spent on administration, (**13**) _____, rental costs + subsidising guest speakers)
Website Information	Updated regularly. Help Desk - The (**14**) _____ of 7 members answers all Help Desk questions. Discussion Forum - members discuss issues together. (Contributors must be members - a (**15**) _____ is supplied on joining)

Questions 16 – 19

*Match the club member (questions **16 - 19**) with her/his actions in the club (**A - F**).*

*Choose **FOUR** letters from the box below, **A - F**, and write them on the answer sheet.*

16   Sally Warner

17   Steven Roth

18   Angela Carter

19   Darren Williamson

Behaviour	
A	Organises insurance for trips.
B	Has just arrived back from a holiday.
C	Lets everyone know the latest club news.
D	Facilitates communication between members.
E	Travels a lot for work.
F	Won't be around for while.

Question 20

*Below is a map of the Edgehill Woods area that the Burley Bird Watching and Nature Club will visit. The four hides that the Club will visit are marked on the map as **A, B, C and D**.*

Please choose the order of the hides that the Club will visit from the possibilities indicated below.

20

- **A**   A - D - B - A
- **B**   A - B - C - D
- **C**   A - C - B - D
- **D**   D - A - C - B

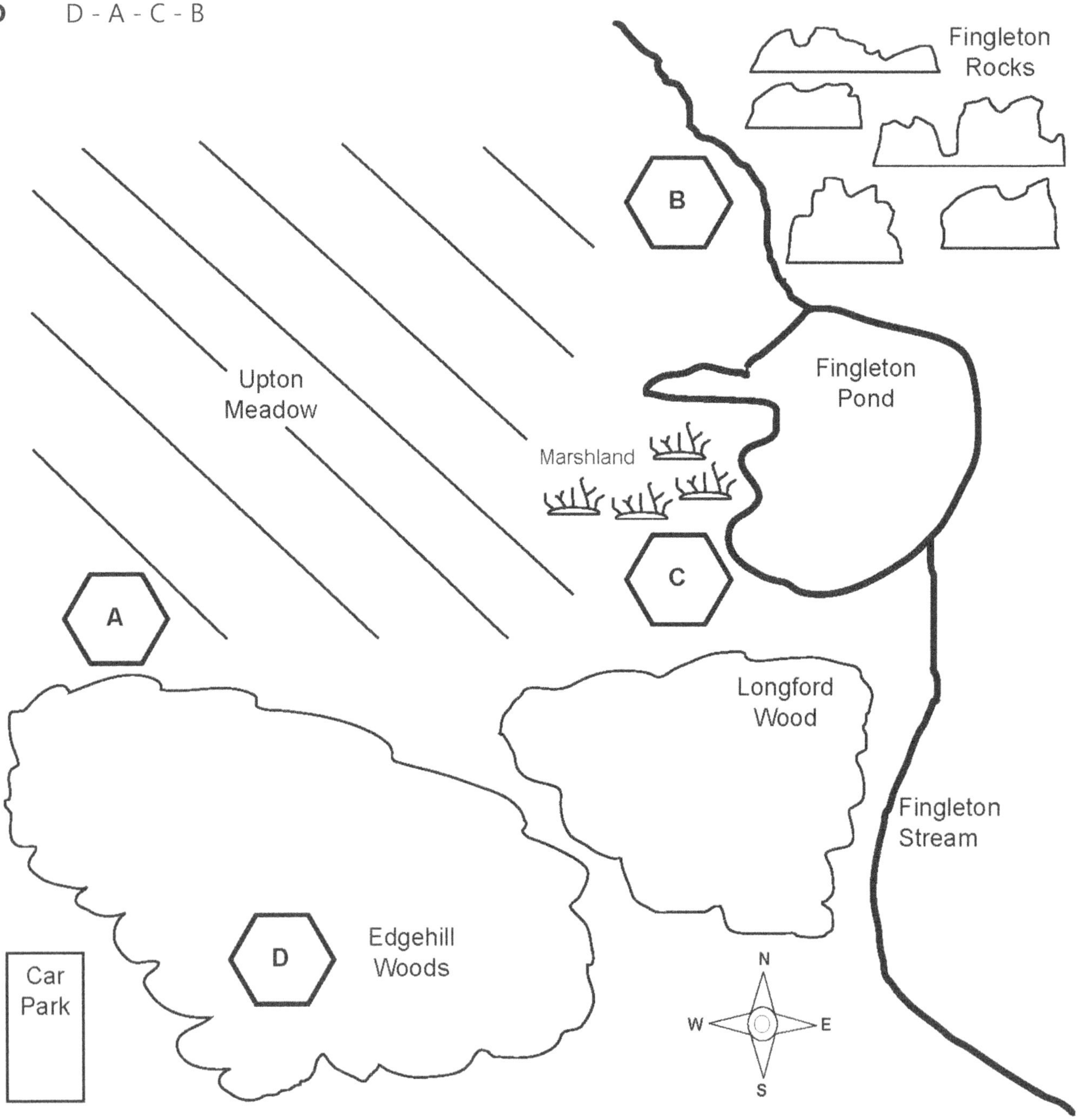

SECTION 3 Questions 21 – 30

Questions 21 – 26

Complete the sentences below.

*Write **NO MORE THAN TWO WORDS** from the listening for each answer.*

21 Mrs. Jones is the _____ at the college.

22 It will be easier to create a cooking area in the empty room, as there were _____ used there.

23 Mike says that the majority of people who bring food eat on the _____ on the campus.

24 Mike says the only major cost for his idea would be the _____ of any outlets in the room.

25 Mrs. Jones said that the only people who would be able to clear up after students during the day would be the _____ and that they would not want to do it.

26 Mrs. Jones said that the café proposal would have no money problems, as it would be _____ in terms of money.

Questions 27 – 30

Answer the questions below.

*Write **NO MORE THAN TWO WORDS** from the listening for each answer.*

27 What does Mrs. Strauss say is currently stored unsafely in the chemistry labs?

28 What is the only security measure at present in each of the science laboratories?

29 What security precaution is already found in the empty room?

30 What does Dr. Cameron ask everyone to give him by Thursday?

SECTION 4   Questions 31 – 40

Questions 31 – 34

Choose the correct letter **A, B or C**.

Write the correct letter in boxes **31 - 34** on your answer sheet.

31   Why is it so difficult to get rid of end of life tyres?

  A   Because of what they are made of.
  B   Because the recycling process releases hazardous chemicals into the surroundings.
  C   Because the methods for processing them are too expensive.

32   Why can't tyre piles be successfully treated with chemicals to destroy mosquitoes?

  A   It's too expensive.
  B   The mosquitoes quickly develop resistance to the chemicals.
  C   The mosquitoes breed too deep in the tyre piles to reach them.

33   What is currently the best way environmentally to extinguish tyre fires?

  A   Let them burn until they go out themselves.
  B   Spray water on them.
  C   Spray fire retardant on them.

34   Why was the tyre fire in Kuwait particularly noteworthy?

  A   The length of time it burned for.
  B   The fire could be seen from space.
  C   It was started deliberately by the military.

Questions 35 – 37

Label the diagram below.

Write **NO MORE THAN TWO WORDS** from the listening for each answer.

Extinguishing Tyre Fires with Liquid Nitrogen

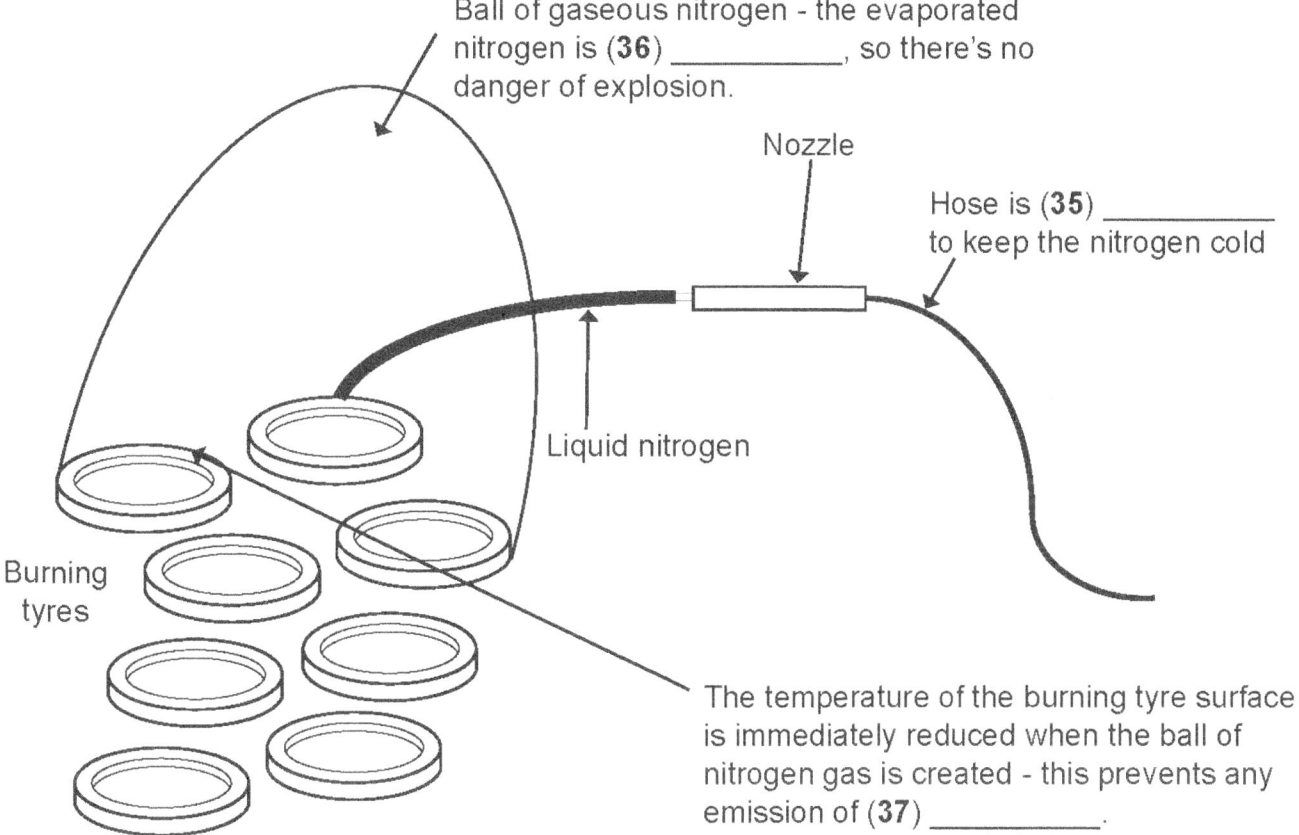

Questions 38 – 40

Complete the notes below.

Write **NO MORE THAN TWO WORDS** from the listening for each answer.

RECYCLING OLD TYRES

Tyres in good condition can be re-moulded and made into re-treads, but usually it's hard to recycle tyres in poor condition. New technology uses (**38**) _____ in the rubber to create a material from which new products can be made; colours and additives can create different indoor and outdoor products with the following advantages:

- durable
- 100% recyclable
- strong

- (**39**) _____ proof
- tough and easy to clean
- water and ultraviolet resistant

Good for making products such as:

- floors
- trailers
- tiles
- wood replacement for building
- ports and extreme condition environments
- children's playgrounds

- running tracks
- artificial sports pitches
- (**40**) _____ for cement kilns
- carpet underlay
- equestrian arenas
- flooring

READING

SECTION 1   Questions 1 – 14

Questions 1 – 7

There are 4 advertisements (**A – D**) for festivals on the next page.

Answer the questions below by writing the letters of the appropriate advertisements (**A – D**) in boxes **1 – 7** on your answer sheet.

1   This advertisement states that the festival is partially dependent on unpaid helpers to be run.

2   This advertisement states that there might be ticket restrictions if people are too young.

3   This advertisement states that it will be only the second time the festival has taken place.

4   This advertisement states that the festival takes place close to the sea.

5   This advertisement states that the festival schedule can now be viewed online.

6   This advertisement states that performers at the festival are selected randomly.

7   This advertisement states that the organisers are not yet sure about everyone who will be performing.

A   Bexington Music Festival

After the success of the inaugural Bexington Food and Music Festival last year, the event is making a return on August 16th this year. Hopefully we'll get the blazing sunshine of last year, which provided the ideal complement to the day's musical entertainment and buzzing street market. The emphasis is on local produce and talent too, with local food suppliers serving up cheeses, artisan breads, cakes, preserves and more, while being serenaded with a full programme of local folk, rock and pop acts. While the musical line-up is yet to be confirmed, it's bound to create a buzz if it's anything like the talent of last year. Little ones will enjoy the entertainment and magic shows by Johnny the Entertainer and all of the town park's popular facilities including the Altitude high-ropes course and outdoor paddling pool will be open for all to enjoy.

B   Bridmouth Arts Festival

The Bridmouth Arts Festival is a rich mix of some of the best regional, national and international arts across dance, film, theatre, performance, visual arts, spoken word, literature and music. The festival brings intriguing, spectacular and (sometimes) down-right curious arts experiences to our town. Visitors will enjoy over 50 events - a spirited mix of dance, film, music, visual art, literature, theatre, comedy and more. Utilising some of Bridmouth's best places and spaces from the traditional to the unexpected. Our Arts by the Ocean Festival extends Bridmouth's popular summer season into an extended summer of arts.

C   Southgate Fringe Theatre Festival

Southgate Theatre Fringe Festival is a four-day Theatre Festival that takes place in Southgate at the end of June. The Southgate Theatre Fringe Festival embraces the widest possible range of theatre forms. Events take place in a variety of circumstances, including venues provided by Southgate Town Council, venues found and equipped by participating companies and many outside locations. The overall aim of the Southgate Theatre Fringe Festival is to provide a low-cost, supportive environment and a level playing field. The festival is not juried or curated – selection is by picking names from a hat for Regular Venues and in order of application for Inside Venues and Outside Performances. No distinction is made as to the status of the companies – amateur, professional, student or whatever. The Southgate Theatre Fringe Festival is supported by a large group of experienced volunteers who provide box-office, stewarding and technical expertise. It attracts invaluable backing from sponsors and grant-giving bodies as well as companies, schools and other institutions that help us in kind.

D   Highcliffe Comedy Festival

The festival is made up of hundreds of shows that take place in Highcliffe between 4th – 6th May this year. Each show has its own capacity depending on the size of the room, which range from 30 – 500 seaters, all of which are located within 10 minutes walk of each other in the centre of town. You only buy a ticket for the show(s) you want to see, allowing you to go and watch as much or as little as you want across the weekend. Shows do sell out, so if there's a show you really want to see, then it is best to buy tickets in advance via the website. If you'd rather take your pick on the weekend, there is a festival box office at the Town Hall selling tickets to all remaining shows. Many of the ticketed shows have an age limit, so it is worth checking before buying tickets for anyone under 18. There are dedicated family shows, including performances for young children. The complete programme is already available on the website.

Questions 8 – 14

Complete the table below.

*Write **NO MORE THAN TWO WORDS** from the text for each answer.*

*Write your answers in boxes **8 - 14** on your answer sheet.*

Post Office Services	
Local Services	
Rent + Council Tax	Allows rent or tax payments by (**8**) _____. Cards or cash can be used.
Home Care	Locals wanting their independence can purchase (**9**) _____ as proof of purchase of a Home Care service.
Meals on Wheels	Locals wanting this service can buy (**10**) _____, which serve as payment.
Government Services	
Motorists	The three (**11**) _____ for renewing a driving licence can be done at the post office.
Passports	People using the passport service are likely to enjoy the better (**12**) _____.
Benefits, Pensions and Tax Credits	Cash can be collected for these services.
Identity Verification	Verification of supporting documents can be conducted.
Foreign Nationals and Residency	Biometrics (which are individuals' distinctive (**13**) _____) can be collected for passport applications and visa applications. Digital version of applicants' fingerprints, faces and (**14**) _____ can also be taken.

Your Local Post Office Services

In addition to the essential products and services we already provide in branch, we're ideally placed to provide easy access to local and national government services on behalf of councils and government departments.

Local Services

We currently deliver essential services on behalf of your local council. As well as in-branch services, we can also support online applications.

Rent and Council Tax Services   An efficient and convenient service managed by local authorities or housing associations. This service lets tenants pay their rent or council tax in nominated Post Office branches using cards or cash.

Home Care   Many local authorities provide Home Care services that help anyone living on their own maintain their independence. Local authorities can sell stamps for these essential services at selected Post Office branches. People simply pop in branch and buy them to show they've bought a Home Care service - simple and effective.

Meals on Wheels   This service is organised at selected Post Office branches on behalf of local authorities in areas where Meals on Wheels is operating. Customers can pop into a branch and purchase vouchers in order to pay for this service.

Government Services

We also provide a range of services for governmental departments and local councils.

Motorists   People can conduct their application, enrolment and identification procedures in order to renew their Photocard Driving Licence for 10 years.

New, Renewal or Replacement Passport   People can use our Passport Check & Send service. Error rates with this service offered at our branches are consistently between 1% and 2%, compared to over 10% for applications sent direct to the Identity and Passport Service.

Benefits, State Pensions and Tax Credit Payments   People can collect their cash using our Post Office Card Accounts and over 3 million currently do.

Identity Verification for the Department of Work & Pensions   If people need verification of their identity as part of the National Insurance application process or need verification of supporting documents like birth and marriage certificates for customers of the pension scheme, we can do this in the Post Office while you wait.

Foreign Nationals and Residency   Foreign nationals applying for residence can now use our advanced biometric data capture booths in around 100 of our branches to enrol their biometrics. Their biometric information is unique characteristics that can be used to identify them. When people apply for a visa or for permission to remain in the UK, we will scan their fingers and thumbs (10 digits) and photograph their face digitally. We'll also capture a digital copy of applicants' signatures and send the application to the Border Agency for approval.

SECTION 2   Questions 15 – 27

Questions 15 – 20

Complete the sentences below.

*Write **NO MORE THAN TWO WORDS** from the text for each answer.*

*Write your answers in boxes **15 - 20** on your answer sheet.*

15   As the _____ of a project is likely to increase during its course, communication needs to be especially reliable.

16   The _____ of delays in points of the critical path can cause missed deadlines.

17   Project leaders should give _____ to their team even when things are going badly.

18   Removing _____ so that a team can work well is a key part of a project manager's job.

19   Exploiting a team's special _____ is an important part of the leadership role in a team.

20   Implementing _____ to ensure that particular team members don't get too far behind can be a useful thing to do.

Better Project Management

Efficient project management is vital to ensure our business runs smoothly. Good project management will guide the project through a visible set of activities and will keep all parties clear about their goals and responsibilities.

Communication is one of the most important skills project managers can have. Without frequent, open and candid communication about goals, obstacles, workarounds and expectations, projects can more easily fail. Priorities and project plans will change, deadlines will be missed, scope will be expanded, but communication must stay consistent. Project managers must work hard to keep lines of communication open to ensure all project stakeholders have all the key details.

Project managers have to be especially skilled at keeping teams and their projects on time and on track. First, create the 'critical path', which is the tasks that need to be done and their particular order. These are the places where projects can get behind and where the cumulative effect is not meeting the project target. It's also important to decide early on the project's clear end-goal and you must also identify a clear definition of what it looks like to achieve the goal. Defining success metrics means measurable goals and a clear finish line for a team.

A project team runs on a solid foundation of trust, mutual respect and accountability, so it's very important to make sure you're fostering an environment where everyone on the team feels heard, their efforts are acknowledged and recognised, and their contributions are valued. Senior executives and customers supporting, and buy-in from other project teams are also critical to the success of projects. This is especially true if things go wrong. And don't save praise only for the times when things are going well - it's almost more important to boost morale through recognising hard work and effort when things don't go as planned - as things don't often go as planned!

One of the most important things a project manager can do is to eliminate obstacles for their teams. That can help keep projects within the agreed-upon framework, make the workflow more efficient and keep everything on schedule. Assign work so it is completed in the most efficient order possible, ensure work that is a predecessor to other work is fully completed before starting another piece, and remove the obstacles that prevent team members from getting their work done. You also should build in extra time around every deadline within a project, to make sure there's plenty of time to resolve the inevitable unexpected problems that will arise. Pay attention to time, cost and where you should be, and how that lines up with your deadlines and project objectives.

Leadership is about helping your project teams succeed and motivating them to persevere. To be a better project manager, you must be intimately familiar with each team member. Familiarise yourself with the unique talents of each person on his team so you know who would and who wouldn't be good for particular jobs. By doing so, you can better predict what challenges may arise and how to overcome them.

Finally, take advantage of the technology available to help you do your job effectively. From project tracking software to file-sharing services to team collaboration tools, find the solution that works best for your teams and put it to work for you. You can also adopt protocols to help keep those chronically late team members on track by building in additional time for approvals.

Questions 21 – 27

Do the following statements agree with the views of the writer of the text?

In boxes 21 – 27 on your answer sheet write:

> **YES** *if the statement agrees with the writer's views*
> **NO** *if the statement doesn't agree the writer's views*
> **NOT GIVEN** *if it is impossible to say what the writer thinks about this*

21   Conducting repeat business is a factor that must be considered when negotiating with a supplier.

22   It's important for your supplier to realise from the start that you too are willing to make compromises in order to achieve a satisfactory deal.

23   Putting pressure on the person you're negotiating with by referring to a deadline that you have to keep can always be a useful negotiation tactic.

24   Getting training with price negotiations can be a very important investment.

25   Research the market of your suppliers' own suppliers to see if prices are falling, as this can make your suppliers' own costs go down.

26   Ensure that your supplier will buy back unused stock at the price that you paid for it.

27   Put as much pressure on your suppliers as possible, as this will help you achieve your goals.

Negotiating with Suppliers

Negotiating the right deal with your suppliers doesn't necessarily mean getting what you want at the cheapest possible price. You may want to negotiate other factors such as delivery times, payment terms or the quality of the goods. Most business owners would view a good deal as one that meets all their requirements. But there are many other issues to consider, such as whether you want to do business with a particular supplier again. Both sides should conclude a negotiation feeling comfortable and happy with the agreement. Negotiations can be unsuccessful if either side feels forced into a corner.

Before you start negotiating, state the aspects of the deal you're happy with and the points you want to discuss. Ask the supplier to do the same. Make sure both sides are satisfied with what is being negotiated. Get the supplier to restate any discounts offered and payment terms. Keep these key bits of information to hand. If you have enough bargaining power, insist on using your own terms and conditions of purchase. Do not indicate that there are things you're prepared to concede or compromise on too early in the negotiations. Try to give the impression you're approaching the negotiations positively without revealing your position. For important or large purchases suggest setting out the key points of the deal in writing. For example, for the purchase of company cars, these might state your requirements, such as the make, year, model, the interior specification and delivery times. If things are in writing, this can help prevent later conflict.

You also need to be aware of common negotiating tactics. If the other party keeps referring to urgent deadlines or a person they need to confer with, remember they may be using pressure tactics. Use such strategies yourself with caution, as they can be very irritating. Don't allow pressure to force you into agreeing to a point you're not happy with. Ask for a break if you need one. Each time you agree to a point, clarify that you've understood it correctly and write it down.

In some trades, suppliers set artificially high prices that are then permanently discounted. If this scenario applies to your business, then ensure that any concessions the supplier gives are real – negotiate discounts that go beyond the standard level.

Some price negotiating techniques will be familiar if you've ever bartered at a market. Never accept the first offer – make a low counter-offer in return. The other party is likely to come back with a revised figure. Always ask what else they can include at the given price. If the price is suspiciously low, ask yourself why. Are the goods of sufficiently high quality? Do they really offer value for money? What will the after-sales service be like?

You can also try to make the asking price look high by exposing any ongoing costs. Ask about repair costs, consumables and other expenses. If the current state of the supplier's market means prices are falling, point this out, as their profit margins will be higher and they'll be able to offer you a better deal.

Use your bargaining power to get a good deal. For example, if you're a big customer of the supplier, you could ask for bulk discounts. But remember that if you squeeze the price too low - perhaps by threatening to walk away from the negotiations - you may end up getting a poor deal. The supplier may have to cut costs elsewhere, maybe in an area such as customer service, which could prove costly to you in the long run. Even if you are a supplier's main customer and enjoy most of the bargaining power, forcing it to meet prices at which it could go out of business won't protect your reputation as a highly valued customer. The supplier will soon look for other customers and is likely to feel resentful.

SECTION 3   Questions 28 – 40

Read the following passage and answer Questions 28 – 40.

Roman Concrete

Ancient Roman concrete has withstood attacks from elements for over 2000 years. Can we learn from the Romans in some way to improve our concrete?

How is it that Roman walls built with their concrete last longer than modern walls? Or is this just a perception? When we build a wall with concrete today, a plywood framework is constructed, concrete is poured into it, and when the concrete is cured, it is removed, leaving the concrete wall. In ancient Rome, two freestanding, parallel walls were built of brick bound with mortar, the combination of which is much, much stronger than plywood. A cavity a couple feet wide was left between the brick walls, and then concrete was poured in, along with some small rocks to bolster stability. This method makes a very sturdy wall. Today, we build buildings to last ten years; the Romans built buildings to last for millennia.

A most unusual Roman structure depicting their technical advancement is the Pantheon. This is a brick faced building constructed to praise the Roman gods and has withstood the ravages of weathering in near perfect condition, sitting magnificently in the business district of Rome. Above all, this building humbles the modern engineer not only in its artistic splendour, but also because there are no steel rods to counter the high tensile forces, such as we need to hold our modern concrete together. Examining this large circular building tells much of the intelligence of its builders; it was designed to contain a fictional ball, and is some 143 feet in diameter with a wall in the form of skirts dropping from its circumference. In the centre of the dome is a 19-foot opening held in place by a bronze ring backed by a brick ring integrated into the concrete dome. This ingenious opening admitted sunlight to brighten the interior and the slightly curved marble floor provided drainage.

Dusty ancient history books teach us that Roman concrete consisted of just three parts: hydrate lime, pozzolan ash from a nearby volcano and a few pieces of fist-sized rock. If these parts were mixed together today in the manner of modern concrete and placed in a structure, the result would certainly not pass the test of the ages. So, how was it that the Romans so many years ago built such elaborate and ageless structures in concrete as seen on the skyline of Rome?

Solving the riddle of ancient concrete is about understanding the chemistry. To understand its chemical composition, we must go back further in time. Three millennia ago, people of the Middle East made walls for their fortifications and homes by pounding moist clay between forms, often called pise work. To protect the surfaces of the clay from erosion, the ancients discovered that a coating of thin, white, burnt limestone would chemically combine with the gases in the air to give a hard protecting and moisture proof shield. We can only guess that the event of discovering this pseudo concrete occurred when a lime coating was applied to a wall made of volcanic, pozzolanic ash near the town of Pozzuoli in Italy. A chemical reaction took place between the chemicals in the wall of volcanic ash (silica and small amounts of alumina and iron oxide) and the layer of lime (calcium hydroxide) applied to the wall. Later, it was found that mixing a little volcanic ash in a fine powder with the moist lime not only made a thicker coat for the ancient concrete, but also produced a durable product that could be submerged in water, something that the plaster product of wet lime and plain sand could not match.

A new concrete product called roller compacted concrete was developed in the last century and this concrete mimics some of ancient concrete's characteristics. Roller compacted concrete consists of a mixture of 40 per cent Portland cement and 60 percent fly ash, a byproduct of electric power plants. By coincidence, the fly ash contains the same amorphous silica compounds as the ash from explosive volcanoes, and, when mixed, the hydrated Portland cement releases the same calcium component recognised in the lime mixing part of the ancient concrete formula. When these two parts were first mixed for roller compacted concrete – for the building of a hydroelectic dam – a bonding gel was formed to tie inert rock pieces together. The calcium hydroxide molecules created in the concrete made with Portland cement and fly ash with amorphous silica can be compared to the composition of the ancient concrete made with wet lime, and volcanic pozzolan with its amorphous silica. Thus, there is a reasonable relationship regarding the concrete components that make the gel for both modern roller compacted concrete and ancient concrete.

The similarity of the ingredients of modern roller compacted concrete and ancient concrete has been explained, but there is more. The ancients hand mixed their components (wet lime and volcanic ash) in a mortar box with very little water to give a nearly dry composition, carried it to the job site in baskets, placing it over a previously prepared layer of rock pieces, and then proceeded to pound the mortar into the rock layer. Is this important? Yes! Close packing of the molecular structure by tamping reduces the need for excess water, which is a source of voids and weakness. In addition, close packing produces more bonding gel than might normally be expected. Again, we have a similarity in the ancient and roller compacted concrete practices, which is little water used and tightly compacting the materials in their placement.

When we review, we can see that the techniques of making ancient concrete have a modern counterpart. The materials (and their ratios) are very similar in both ancient and modern roller compacted concrete and the technique of tamping stiff mortar into the voids of a rock layer to avoid empty spaces are also common to both.

Questions 28 – 30

Label the diagram below.

Write **NO MORE THAN THREE WORDS** from the text for each answer.

Write your answers in boxes **28 - 30** on your answer sheet.

Roman Walls and Modern Walls

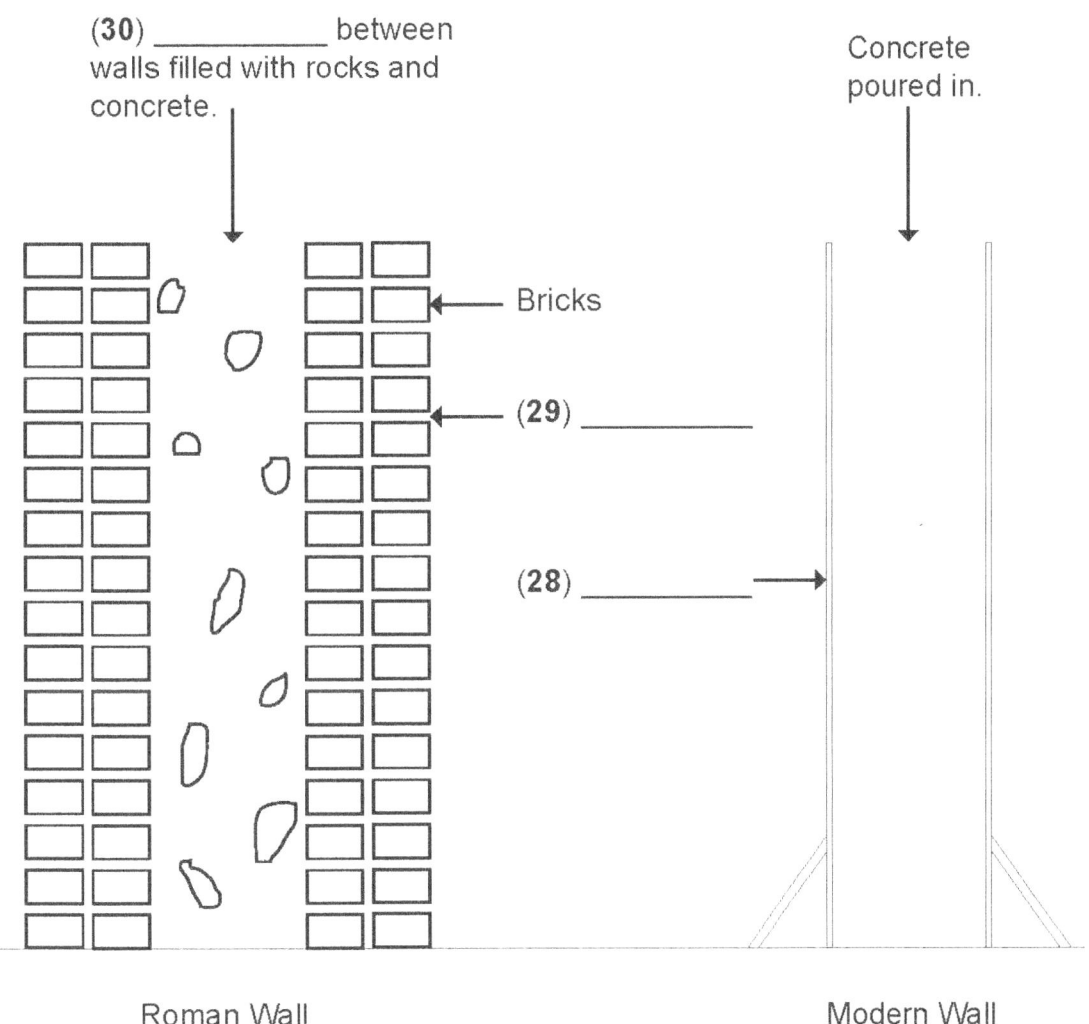

Questions 31 – 36

Do the following statements agree with the information given in the text?

In boxes 31 – 36 on your answer sheet write:

> **TRUE** *if the statement agrees with the information*
> **FALSE** *if the statement contradicts the information*
> **NOT GIVEN** *if there is no information on this*

31 The Pantheon was constructed for business purposes.

32 When it was first built, light could not penetrate the Pantheon.

33 Pozzolan ash from volcanoes was difficult to mine for the ancients.

34 The limestone coating on ancient concrete created a water-resistant layer.

35 Using a little volcanic ash in the composition of ancient concrete allowed its use under water.

36 Electricity generation was inadvertently very useful in helping make the ingredients for roller compacted concrete.

Questions 37 – 40

*Choose **FOUR** letters, **A - G**.*

According to the text, which of the following are true for both Roman concrete and roller compacted concrete?

*Write the correct letter, **A - G**, in any order in boxes 37 - 40 on your answer sheet.*

A The compositions of both concretes were discovered by accident.

B Both concretes contain amorphous silica compounds.

C Sulphuric acid derivatives are required in the composition of both concretes.

D Both concretes release a calcium component during their composition.

E Both concretes require little water in their composition.

F Both concretes dry quickly, even in wet conditions.

G Packing techniques used for making both concretes reduce the threat of vulnerable gaps in the finished product.

WRITING

WRITING TASK 1

You should spend about 20 minutes on this task.

> **You are on holiday and you have realised that you will soon have a delivery of a package to be left at your door.**
>
> **Write a letter to your neighbour. In your letter,**
>
> - **tell him/her that you are on holiday and say where you are**
> - **explain the problem that you have regarding the package that will be delivered**
> - **say when you will return and retrieve the package**

You should write at least 150 words.

*You do **NOT** need to write any addresses. Begin your letter as follows:*

> *Dear John / Jane,*

WRITING TASK 2

You should spend about 40 minutes on this task.

Write about the following topic:

> **Having a salaried job is better than being self-employed.**
>
> **To what extent do you agree or disagree?**

Give reasons for your answer and include any relevant examples from your knowledge or experience.

You should write at least 250 words.

SPEAKING

PART 1

- Can you tell me a little about when you were a child?
- What was it like for you when you first went to school?
- What are some of things you did when you were at your first school?

Topic 1   Credit Cards
- Do you ever use a credit card? (Why?/Why not?)
- What are some of the dangers about using a credit card?
- Do you think cards will ever replace cash? (Why?/Why not?)
- Do you think a payment system on a phone or watch will ever replace cards? (Why?/Why not?)

Topic 2   Change
- Are you someone who likes change? (Why?/Why not?)
- How have you changed over the years?
- How has your country changed over the last 20 years?
- What in your opinion needs to change in today's world?

PART 2

> Describe a favourite relative that you have.
> You should say:
>
> who this relative is
> how often you see this relative
> what you do/did with this relative when you see/saw each other
>
> and explain why this relative is a favourite of yours.

PART 3

Topic 1   Relationships
- What are some of the strongest relationships you've had in your life?
- How are family relationships different to friend relationships?
- In what ways are today's relationships different to what they were like 30 years ago?
- How do you feel about romantic relationships that begin online?

Topic 2   Homelessness
- What do you think are some of the causes of homelessness?
- What happens in your country to help homeless people?
- Do you think homelessness will increase in the future or not? (Why?/Why not?)
- Do you think restaurants should donate unused food at the end of the day to homeless people? (Why?/Why not?)

Listening Test Answer Sheet

1		21	
2		22	
3		23	
4		24	
5		25	
6		26	
7		27	
8		28	
9		29	
10		30	
11		31	
12		32	
13		33	
14		34	
15		35	
16		36	
17		37	
18		38	
19		39	
20		40	

Reading Test Answer Sheet

1		21	
2		22	
3		23	
4		24	
5		25	
6		26	
7		27	
8		28	
9		29	
10		30	
11		31	
12		32	
13		33	
14		34	
15		35	
16		36	
17		37	
18		38	
19		39	
20		40	

Answers

LISTENING ANSWERS

/ indicates an alternative answer   ( ) indicates an optional answer

TEST 21	TEST 22	TEST 23	TEST 24	TEST 25
1. Stuart	1. Fuller	1. Griffiths	1. insurance	1. W74
2. 6FR	2. 1998	2. GH6	2. 12	2. March
3. 645	3. 85	3. 375	3. email	3. Friday
4. cash	4. unlimited minutes	4. 5	4. offer	4. wiring
5. brakes	5. cash	5. 4th	5. 118	5. 4
6. 7	6. 6	6. (ID) badge / ID (badge)	6. routine	6. bandwidth
7. log book	7. supervisor	7. social security number	7. diagnosis	7. 70
8. Wednesday	8. bicycle	8. rolls	8. 10,000	8. 2 years
9. 200	9. gloves	9. project	9. bite	9. engineer
10. B	10. valuables	10. swipe	10. monthly payments	10. X49
11. Patients	11. A	11. food chain	11. planner	11. 1962
12. (The) admission letter	12. B	12. (The) elevation	12. fee	12. joining fee
13. Emergencies	13. C	13. Herbs	13. bookings	13. insurance
14. (By) telephone	14. B	14. Farming	14. injury	14. committee
15. Medication	15. D	15. Charcoal	15. first aid kit	15. password
16. A	16. G	16. F	16. routes	16. C
17. C	17. A	17. E	17. goggles	17. F
18. eye unit	18. H	18. A	18. traffic	18. A
19. (The) pharmacy	19. B	19. G	19. winter	19. D
20. (The) information point	20. E	20. C	20. challenge	20. C
21. Seaboards	21. experiments	21. A	21. B*	21. site manager
22. (A) rift	22. Research methods	22. B	22. C*	22. gas appliances
23. Sediment	23. Health	23. B	23. D*	23. grass
24. 70%	24. options	24. C	24. F*	24. decommissioning
25. Blood	25. scientific aspects	25. A	25. H*	25. caretakers
26. surface temperature	26. motivation	26. B	26. nutrients	26. self-sufficient
27. minerals	27. supervisor	27. F	27. sewage	27. chemicals
28. Oxygen	28. prize	28. (The) router	28. concentrations	28. dead locks
29. outlet	29. self-discipline	29. (A) bell	29. temperate regions	29. shutters
30. evaporation	30. literature review	30. (A) deposit	30. D	30. proposals
31. protection	31. decline	31. B	31. shallow	31. A
32. habitat	32. Forecasts	32. A	32. technology	32. C
33. temperate	33. quality of life	33. A	33. efficiency	33. A
34. latitude	34. speed	34. C	34. A*	34. B
35. fat	35. surface traffic	35. average car	35. C*	35. insulated
36. (curative) power	36. fuel	36. constraint	36. D*	36. non-combustible
37. prey	37. alternative	37. low speed profile	37. F*	37. (toxic) gases
38. genetic diversity	38. cooperation	38. insulation	38. (A) (steel) support	38. (nano) particles
39. immune systems	39. Smoke number	39. (the) charge controller	39. (A) (wind) sensor	39. corrosion
40. educational programmes	40. First order approximation	40. (the) inverter	40. (A) gearbox	40. fuel
			Note: * Answers for qu. 21–25 and 34-37: these answers in any order.	

ANSWERS

IELTS 5 Practice Tests, General Set 5

READING ANSWERS

/ indicates an alternative answer ( ) indicates an optional answer

TEST 21	TEST 22	TEST 23	TEST 24	TEST 25
1. E	1. The club policy	1. The interactive consoles	1. D	1. C
2. C	2. A walking service	2. Book online	2. E	2. D
3. B	3. A chillout zone	3. The salad bars	3. A	3. A
4. A	4. The Playworker	4. Departure boards	4. B	4. B
5. E	5. Lunch	5. (Internet-connected) PC's	5. C	5. D
6. D	6. The discount rate	6. The receipt	6. D	6. C
7. B	7. The Club Leader	7. validity	7. B	7. A
8. nomination	8. NOT GIVEN	8. fodder	8. chain	8. tenants
9. joining pack	9. TRUE	9. age restrictions	9. alarm	9. stamps
10. independent judge	10. TRUE	10. reception	10. Neighbours	10. vouchers
11. syllabus	11. NOT GIVEN	11. Approval	11. Research	11. procedures
12. constitution	12. TRUE	12. TRUE	12. trash	12. error rates
13. categories	13. FALSE	13. FALSE	13. motion sensor	13. characteristics
14. verification	14. FALSE	14. FALSE	14. postcode	14. signatures
15. TRUE	15. misunderstandings	15. NO	15. traffic	15. scope
16. TRUE	16. purpose	16. NO	16. buffer	16. cumulative effect
17. NOT GIVEN	17. competition	17. YES	17. default	17. praise
18. TRUE	18. regulations	18. YES	18. code	18. obstacles
19. FALSE	19. conventions	19. YES	19. antivirus software	19. talents
20. NOT GIVEN	20. accessibility	20. NOT GIVEN	20. privileges	20. protocols
21. FALSE	21. ranking	21. YES	21. administrative account	21. YES
22. B*	22. D	22. E	22. stock	22. NO
23. C*	23. F	23. C	23. expanding businesses	23. NO
24. F*	24. B	24. A	24. overheads	24. NOT GIVEN
25. G*	25. E	25. F	25. Order forms	25. YES
26. I*	26. A	26. E	26. Overdrafts	26. NOT GIVEN
27. J*	27. C	27. D	27. finance providers	27. NO
28. sewage	28. iv	28. AW	28. lifestyles	28. A plywood framework
29. bacteria	29. vi	29. AE	29. acute	29. Mortar
30. hypoxia	30. x	30. PR	30. burden	30. A cavity
31. seasonal	31. vii	31. SK	31. lower productivity	31. FALSE
32. degradation	32. i	32. SA	32. families	32. FALSE
33. catchment area	33. viii	33. TM	33. investigation	33. NOT GIVEN
34. food chain	34. iii	34. PR	34. psychological factors	34. TRUE
35. fish gills	35. C	35. AE	35. quality of life	35. TRUE
36. recreational	36. B	36. bees	36. socio-economic	36. TRUE
37. Research	37. D	37. fermentation	37. C	37. B*
38. benefits	38. C	38. drying	38. D	38. D*
39. Energy	39. E	39. B	39. B	39. E*
40. education	40. A	40. C	40. C	40. G*
Note:*Answers for qu. 23 - 27 in any order				Note:*Answers for qu. 37 - 40 in any order

READING ANSWERS HELP

This section shows fragments of passages that contain the correct answers. If you have trouble locating the correct answer in the text, or can't understand why a particular answer is correct, refer to this section to understand the reasoning behind the answers. A group of answers with answers being preceded by * means that this group of answers may be given in any order. Answers in brackets () are optional answers.

GENERAL READING TEST 21

1. **E** Check out our new extension!

2. **C** Local really does mean local – all the produce must be grown, reared, caught or processed by the stall holder and all within a 30-mile radius of the market.

3. **B** Lunchtime specials available Mon - Fri, 11.00 - 14.3

4. **A** To trade at Tradewise Cash and Carry, you must be a business or a charity. Membership is free. All customers must be over 18. An email address is required to complete your registration.

5. **E** *Booking recommended!*

6. **D** with a focus on ethical and environmental practices.

7. **B** *Please note that from 13th November we'll be closed for one week for renovations.*

8. **nomination** Applying for membership is easy. Download and print the nomination and lodge it with one of the committee members.

9. **joining pack** Also required is a once-only joining fee of twelve dollars that covers the costs of the joining pack.

10. **independent judge** An independent judge scores and provides feedback on all entries.

11. **syllabus** Among the club's key objectives is the ongoing education of its members. Our syllabus is designed to extend and challenge members' talents and abilities.

12. **constitution** According to our constitution, all the posts on the club's committees have to change regularly

13. **categories** Inside each forum there can be different categories related to the forum topic

14. **verification** After verification of your club membership, your email address will be added to the distribution list, and you will receive a welcome message via email.

15. **TRUE** Monitoring shouldn't be excessive and must be reasonably justified.

16. **TRUE** In some sectors, employers may have a legal or regulatory need to carry out some monitoring.

17. **NOT GIVEN** There is nothing in the text relating to this and so the answer is 'not given' in the text.

18. **TRUE** Employers should have procedures in place setting out what is and isn't allowed. Some websites may be banned or marked as at risk.

19. **FALSE** Workers must also be given the reason for the monitoring.

20. **NOT GIVEN** There is nothing in the text relating to this and so the answer is 'not given' in the text.

21. **FALSE** It's very rare that employers would need to carry out covert monitoring without the staff being told they are being monitored, but they can do it.

22. **B*** Your competitor could be a new business offering a substitute or similar product that makes your own redundant – keep an eye out on advertising, which is where this information often appears.

23. **C*** If your competitor is a public company, read a copy of their annual report. Limited companies have to lodge their accounts with Companies House.

24. **F*** Use a search engine to track down similar products.

25. **G*** Make the most of contacts with your customers. Ask which of your competitors they buy from and how you compare.

26. **I*** Use meetings with your suppliers to ask what their other customers are doing.

27. **J*** It's also likely you'll meet competitors at social and business events. Talk to them. Be friendly - they're competitors, not enemies. You'll probably share common problems. You'll get a better idea of them - and you might need each other one day, for example in collaborating to grow a new market for a new product.

28. **sewage** The major nutrient sources are fertilisers, sewage, and the burning of fossil fuels.

29. **bacteria** When these algae die and sink to the bottom of the sea, they provide a rich food source for bacteria, which in the act of decomposition consume dissolved oxygen from the surrounding waters.

30. **hypoxia** Shallow waters are much less likely to stratify compared to deep waters, and are thus less liable to develop hypoxia.

31. **seasonal** About half of the hypoxic zones around the world are seasonal, as oxygen depletion occurs in spring and summer following the increase in phytoplankton that results from nutrient enrichment. These hypoxic zones usually last from a few weeks to several months; however, in some locations, about 8 per cent of worldwide hypoxic conditions occur continuously throughout the year.

32. **degradation**   As human populations increase and the land suffers further degradation, requiring more and more fertiliser, dead zones will become more commonplace. For example, every year now, near where the Mississippi River goes into the sea, large dead zones form of 22,000 square kilometres.

33. **catchment area**   Farming using excessive nitrogen fertilisers in the river's catchment area is blamed for this and a plan has been formulated to reduce dead zones by 30 per cent over the next 3 years.

34. **food chain**   These harmful algal blooms release toxins that contaminate drinking water, causing illnesses for animals and humans. After being consumed by small fish and shellfish, these toxins move up the food chain and can hurt bigger animals like sea lions, turtles, dolphins, birds, manatees, and fish.

35. **fish gills**   Even if algal blooms are not toxic, they can hurt aquatic life by obstructing the sunlight and clogging fish gills.

36. **recreational**   Algal blooms and dead zones also have less obvious effects. Economists have examined the effects of nutrient overenrichment on both market goods, primarily commercial fisheries, and nonmarket industries, primarily recreational.

37. **Research**   Although many aquatic ecosystems have yet to be properly studied in this regard, there is plenty of research that shows how much impact dead zones have had on these two economic spheres.

38. **benefits**   For example, it's been recently shown that there would be considerable benefits in terms of the economy to reducing nitrogen loading and hypoxic conditions in the Baltic Sea, which is an area that has long suffered dead zones caused by these problems.

39. **Energy**   A more fundamental effect of hypoxia is the loss of energy from the ocean. By precluding or stunting the growth of bottom-dwellers such as clams and worms, hypoxia robs their predators of an important source of nutrition. For example, scientists estimate that Chesapeake Bay in the United States loses about 10,000 metric tons of energy to hypoxia each year, 5 per cent of the Bay's total production of food energy. The Baltic Sea has lost 30 per cent of its food energy – a condition that has contributed to the significant decline in its fisheries' yields.

40. **education**   In order to improve the situation, a variety of action is required, including regulatory programs, the education of the various areas of society that are in any way involved and the provision of support, including financial commitments, to ensure that the programs and education takes place effectively and successfully.

ANSWERS　　　　　　　　　　　　　　　　　　　　　IELTS 5 Practice Tests, General Set 5

GENERAL READING TEST 22

1. **The club policy**　　　The club policy ensures that the enthusiastic, fun and caring approach to the needs of your child will create a safe and enjoyable experience.

2. **A walking service**　　　We are based in the new Sports Pavilion at the town's Junior School, with a walking service offered for the children who attend the local Infants School.

3. **A chillout zone**　　　In addition, we have a chillout zone where the children can chat and read comics.

4. **The Playworker**　　　the Playworker looking after your group will take your child into the play area and help them settle in (especially on their first day).

5. **Lunch**　　children should please bring lunch.

6. **The discount rate**　　　Early bookings help us to plan more exciting trips and activities and we would like to encourage you to take advantage of the discount rate by doing this.

7. **The Club Leader**　　　parents should liaise with the Club Leader regarding estimated collection times.

8. **NOT GIVEN**　　　There is nothing in the text relating to this and so the answer is 'not given' in the text.

9. **TRUE**　　Many schools can attend from their classrooms via the latest digital technology.

10. **TRUE**　　Gallery Ticket　Explore for free our permanent galleries showcasing the best of the museum's collection.

11. **NOT GIVEN**　　　There is nothing in the text relating to this and so the answer is 'not given' in the text.

12. **TRUE**　　on hot days we close all vessels when the temperature reaches 36° Celsius to ensure visitor safety.

13. **FALSE**　　We're upgrading our visitor experience during February when the museum will be undergoing renovations. Our foyer will be temporarily closed for February, with our ticket office relocated to the side of the museum closest to Murray Street. Our staff will be available to help you find your way.

14. **FALSE**　　bring your own picnic lunch to eat on the museum's harbour-side terrace.

15. **misunderstandings**　　　Constructing an effective website without a plan is like constructing a building without blueprints. Things end up in the wrong place, features are overlooked, and the situation is ripe for miscommunication between website developer and client.

16. **purpose** Because planning is so essential when it comes to designing a website, start by identifying the exact rationale for having a site. Typical reasons why businesses develop websites include building brand awareness, finding new customers, saving money, selling products and providing improved customer support. We recommend that you write down what you want to do with your website.

17. **competition** If you are unsure about what you want, then check out companies working in the same sector as you or other websites for inspiration. Once you establish what you want your website to accomplish, look at your prospective audience. This can include your current and potential customers, new prospects, stakeholders, suppliers and partners.

18. **regulations** When you are planning content for your site, don't forget you are legally required to publish certain company information.

19. **conventions** A standard navigation bar that is in the same place on every page enables the user to move quickly through the site. Follow established web practices for navigation - this will help make your website more intuitive for the user.

20. **accessibility** While you are making sure that your website is consistent and true to your brand, don't forget - it also needs to be easy to use.

21. **ranking** Search engines now grade content based on how well it appears on mobile devices.

22. **D** If you negotiate a contract, you don't have to wait until the end of your contract to begin a new one or get a better deal. Energy prices can change throughout the year, so consider negotiating on a low priced day or when the market prices are going down.

23. **F** When negotiating your contract, it's important to consider any major developments you plan for your business. If you plan to expand your operations, consider a shorter contract until you have a better idea of the energy you'll need.

24. **B** Enquire about details on pricing and any discounts with an offer, such as pay on time discounts.

25. **E** In a rising market, where current prices are cheaper than future prices, it may be better to choose a longer contract. In a decreasing market, it may be better to select a short period, with the aim of buying cheaper in the future.

26. **A** Aim to give them at least 12 months of data showing your energy use for each half-hour period. This will show them your peak, shoulder and off-peak usage and your maximum demand, which may influence the network charges that you pay.

27. **C** When you're shopping around, make sure you bear in mind any broker or exit fees in your comparison.

28. **iv** Various information within Paragraph A.

29. **vi** Various information within Paragraph B.

ANSWERS

30. **x** Various information within Paragraph C.

31. **vii** Various information within Paragraph D.

32. **i** Various information within Paragraph E.

33. **viii** Various information within Paragraph F.

34. **iii** Various information within Paragraph G.

35. **C** England's letters of safe conduct were first written in Latin and English, but in 1772, the government decided to use the international language of high finance and diplomacy: French.

36. **B** The passport returned, however, during the First World War in an effort to reduce espionage. As a result, Britain produced the first recognisably modern passport as a single page, folded into eight, with a cardboard cover, a photograph of the bearer and a note of such details as shape of face and features.

37. **D** Although passports are important for the citizens of every country, the utility of some passports can be seen as greater than others. One method to measure the 'value' of a passport is to calculate its 'visa-free score,' which is the number of countries that allow the holder of that passport entry for general tourism without requiring a visa.

38. **C** This leads to vastly less queuing required at airports, which is what is perceived as the greatest benefit of this system.

39. **E** Because many countries, for example the U.S., don't issue any other form of national identification card, carrying a passport has become a way for citizens to assume a national identity.

40. **A** When biometric passports were introduced, the International Civil Aviation Organisation decided the key should consist of, in this particular order: the passport number; the owner's date of birth; the passport expiry date. As a result of this sequence, the key was soon cracked with a reader people can buy in shops for only two hundred dollars.

GENERAL READING TEST 23

1. **The interactive consoles**   If you don't want to just browse, take advantage of the interactive consoles that will give you details of all our stores.

2. **Book online**   Lounge access is always subject to availability, so it's advised to book online to ensure you're not disappointed.

3. **The salad bars**   Take advantage of the salad bars (available on the house with a purchased main meal) at both restaurants.

4. **Departure boards**   In all eating areas, you will have view of departure boards, giving you up-to-date information on your flight.

5. **(Internet-connected) PC's**   Need to be online while you're on the move? You can work, browse and keep in touch via wireless broadband or using Internet-connected PC's.

6. **The receipt**   Please have the receipt if you wish to take advantage of this service.

7. **validity**   When you leave the Zoological Gardens, your ticket's validity will expire.

8. **fodder**   Although animals may often appear to be tame and may win our affection when begging for food, their welfare and health can only be ensured when they are exclusively fed using the fodder of the zoo.

9. **age restrictions**   Parents must be aware of the age restrictions, which must be strictly observed when using the play equipment, the playgrounds of the petting zoo and similar facilities.

10. **reception**   Lost and found items must also be handed in to the Zoo staff at the reception, where they can be picked up.

11. **Approval**   Please appreciate that the publication of photographs or film segments from the Zoo as well as photographs or films taken to make money require our approval.

12. **TRUE**   All services starting from the Eddison Road bus station will now start at a line of temporary bus stops next to the Parkstone Playing Fields. Unfortunately, there will be no covered waiting area at this location. This temporary change will lead to all services arriving 4 minutes later than their usual scheduled time.

13. **FALSE**   These new arrangements are initially for approximately one year and are subject to alteration for operational reasons.

14. **FALSE**   All town night bus services will run later that night until 4 a.m. in order to help people get home safely and cheaply.

15. **NO**   The biggest monetary benefit to the company from owning a business car is the cost savings from tax deductions.

16. **NO** — For the employee, the cost of the car as an asset is not deductible (even for interest expenses on borrowing money to buy the car).

17. **YES** — If the business owns the car, personal use of the car by the employee must be documented and the company must report personal use as taxable compensation

18. **YES** — Insurance for a company-owned car will probably be cheaper than for an employee-owned vehicle, since businesses can get leased-car and multiple-car rates and other discounts

19. **YES** — it's nearly always the case that leased cars should be privileges for owners and executives

20. **NOT GIVEN** — There is nothing in the text relating to this and so the answer is 'not given' in the text.

21. **YES** — Aside from the significant benefits for recruitment and retention, the value of a company car programme to an organisation is only truly understood when it is not there or something goes wrong.

22. **E** — document the meeting and outcomes.

23. **C** — It's important to understand the difference between underperformance and serious misconduct. The latter is when an employee causes serious and imminent risk to the health and safety of another person or to the reputation or profits of their employer's business, or deliberately behaves in a way that's inconsistent with continuing their employment.

24. **A** — The best businesses are always improving their operations to stay competitive in their sector.

25. **F** — Where performance has improved, employers should make sure they appreciate this.

26. **E** — It's important to be clear about what could happen and what the employee's responsibilities are. This can also help prevent employees feeling they're being picked on if an issue does come up.

27. **D** — The best way to manage underperformance is to make sure it doesn't happen in the first place.

28. **AW** — According to eco-farming lecturer Anna Winter, "the production of artificial vanillin creates a stream of wastewater that requires treatment before it can be released into surface water. Catalysts currently used in the manufacturing of vanillin are also polluting and can only be used one time."

29. **AE** — Farmer Alex Ellis explains. + It's at this stage, when the beans start to change from green to brown, that they start to develop aroma."

30. **PR** — Patricia Roberts says it's necessary to assess the vanilla bean before our purchase. "You should be able to take a bean, tie it around your finger, and untie it. That's how supple a good vanilla bean should be.

31. **SK**   Botanist Sylvia Karner explains that these wonderful attributes have created a different industry. "The most prominent of the components is vanillin, which can be artificially made from petrochemicals and from eugenol, a component of clove oil. As total worldwide vanilla production is only about 2000 metric tons, this does not satisfy demand.

32. **SA**   "When prices for cured beans drop due to price speculation or an increased global supply," economist Salim Aziz explains, "farmers tear up crops. They can't afford to keep growing vanilla when prices stay so low."

33. **TM**   "Vanilla requires a fair amount of skill to grow," explains Tom McCullum, co-founder of a direct-trade chocolate and vanilla company. "You can't just put seed in the ground, tend to it and expect it to produce a yield. Hand pollination is a learned skill. Many farmers have been growing vanilla for three to four generations. Smallholder farmers have an absolute sixth sense as to when the orchids will bloom."

34. **PR**   "Vanilla's price volatility is historic," says Patricia Roberts, a dealer in vanilla. "In part, it is the result of cycles of tropical storms, something that may change in unpredictable ways due to climate change."

35. **AE**   "This usually occurs indoors, in a well-ventilated room where beans are placed on racks," Ellis says.

36. **bees**   Vanilla in its native habitat is pollinated by bees. Each flower remains open for just 24 hours, after which, if not pollinated, it wilts, dies, and drops to the ground. In terms of farming it, this means that vanilla flowers need to be hand-pollinated.

37. **fermentation**   They are then blanched in hot water to halt fermentation

38. **drying**   a process that ends with a period of slow drying.

39. **B**   Vanilla beans start to ferment as soon as they are harvested, so there is an urgent need for farmers to find buyers for their beans.

40. **C**   A decade ago, the prices for green beans dropped to 20 dollars a kilo and remained there for 5 years. The following price increase was built on speculation that, due to poor pollination, the vanilla crop would be small.

ANSWERS

GENERAL READING TEST 24

1. **D**   get instant cover online today.

2. **E**   Do you want to wake up every morning in a new place?

3. **A**   The other three have panoramic views of the mountains that rise behind us.

4. **B**   Indoor and outdoor play areas for children

5. **C**   We can also provide a meet and greet service at the airport, train or bus station and drive you to your destination in comfort.

6. **D**   No upper age limits!

7. **B**   Hot showers, cooking and washing-up facilities, launderette, electric hook ups and TV connections are all standard at all our sites or pitches.

8. **chain**   Keep the chain on when answering the door and don't allow anyone into your home that you don't know.

9. **alarm**   Burglars don't like noise, so getting a dog is always a good way to scare them off. If getting a dog is not practical for you, then installing an alarm is a must.

10. **Neighbours**   A great way to ward off unwanted visitors and potential burglars is to get friendly with neighbours, so that everyone can help each other out. This is especially helpful when/if you go on vacation for an extended period of time and need someone to help you keep a close eye on your property.

11. **Research**   Thieves will frequent dark areas because it's easier for them to watch and conduct research for their burglaries and run away and not get caught. Having light around your home at night will keep your area well lit and more likely clear of criminals.

12. **trash**   Some criminals will go through your trash to see what you've left behind. For example, if you recently bought an expensive TV and are throwing out the packaging, a criminal who sees that might use it as a clue and incentive to come back and find a way to get the TV.

13. **motion sensor**   Another modern device is the motion sensor, which is great for detecting movement. When armed, it will turn on bright lights and send a message to your mobile device if it detects something.

14. **postcode**   Write your postcode on items like televisions in your house with an invisible ultraviolet ink pen. This will make your property easier to trace if it's found and it will also make your property harder to sell on.

15. **traffic**   The first thing you should do is to use a firewall to secure your Internet connection. This can analyse traffic to see if it should be allowed onto your network.

16. **buffer** — Or, if you have a more complicated set up with many different types of devices, you might require a dedicated system. The firewall effectively creates a buffer between your IT network and other, external networks, which in the simplest case means between your computer (or computers) and 'the Internet'.

17. **default** — Manufacturers often set the default of new software and devices to be as open and multi-functional as possible. They come with 'everything on' to make them easily connectable and usable. Unfortunately, this can also provide cyber attackers with opportunities to gain unauthorised access to your data, often without difficulty.

18. **code** — For 'important' accounts, such as banking and IT administration, you should use two-factor authentication, also known as 2FA. A common and effective example of this involves a code delivered to a smartphone that you must enter in addition to your password.

19. **antivirus software** — Antivirus software is often included for free within popular operating systems, so it should be used on all computers and laptops.

20. **privileges** — To minimise the potential damage that could be done if an account is misused or stolen, staff should have just enough privileges to software, settings, online services and device connectivity functions for them to perform their role.

21. **administrative account** — By ensuring as well that your staff don't browse the web from an administrative account, you cut down on the chance that it will be compromised. This is important because an attacker with unauthorised access to an administrative account can be far more damaging than one accessing a standard user account.

22. **stock** — You should measure your production efficiency and the quantity and quality of the stock you hold and produce to ensure you can meet all your orders in a way that satisfies your customers.

23. **expanding businesses** — overtrading can be a danger for many businesses. Overtrading is an imbalance between the work that a business takes on and its capacity to do the work. This can happen when a business takes on work, but cannot live up to the resulting demands. This is particularly common in expanding businesses

24. **overheads** — Many cash flow problems also arise from too many overheads.

25. **Order forms** — You should also ensure order forms are clear and easy to use to improve the sales and payment processes.

26. **Overdrafts** — Overdrafts for example can see you through temporarily.

27. **finance providers** — Having a cash flow forecast to demonstrate the shortfall is temporary will reassure finance providers.

28. **lifestyles** — Sedentary lifestyles can also set the stage for back pain, especially when a weekday routine of getting too little exercise is punctuated by a strenuous weekend workout.

29. acute Most back pain is acute and lasts from a few days to a few weeks, however, it can become chronic.

30. burden Back pain is the leading cause of activity limitation and work absence throughout much of the world, imposing an extreme economic burden on individuals, families, communities, industry, and governments.

31. lower productivity In the United States, an estimated 149 million work days are lost every year because of back pain, with total costs estimated to be a hundred billion to two hundred billion dollars a year, of which two-thirds is due to lower productivity.

32. families Approximately 35 per cent of the financial expenses related to back pain are for services provided in the private sector and thus are most likely paid for directly by patients and their families.

33. investigation 7 per cent to medication, 6 per cent to community care and 5 per cent to radiology and imaging used for investigation.

34. psychological factors As well as the loss of their own work, unpaid carers are a group that creates loss of work due to the physical and psychological factors involved and they themselves often present to healthcare services as secondary patients.

35. quality of life Whatever the different impacts of back pain are, the estimates of the economic burden of chronic back pain do not do justice to the extent of suffering and decreased quality of life experienced by patients.

36. socio-economic Thus, although the wider impacts of chronic back pain - in terms of suffering and impact on quality of life - are impossible to quantify with any degree of precision, it is clear that they come at a high price in terms of an individual's physical, psychological, and social well-being. Of course, on top of all this, society does pay the financial price of treatment and it also suffers the lost work of the sufferers and carers. Back pain is an affliction that has diverse socio-economic impacts at many different levels.

37. C Unpaid carers actually save countries enormous amounts of money. Last year, the work of unpaid carers saved the UK National Health Service up to 119 billion pounds

38. D it becomes a permanent feature of their lives and its effects on well-being can be wide reaching, leading to depression, sleep disturbance and fatigue, decrements in physical and cognitive functioning, and changes in mood, personality, and social interactions of the sufferer.

39. B the wider impacts of chronic back pain - in terms of suffering and impact on quality of life - are impossible to quantify with any degree of precision

40. C This is a holistic answer and involves synthesis of the whole text. This text in its entirety fits "The Costs of Back Pain" better than the other three answers.

GENERAL READING TEST 25

1. **C** The Southgate Theatre Fringe Festival is supported by a large group of experienced volunteers

2. **D** Many of the ticketed shows have an age limit, so it is worth checking before buying tickets for anyone under 18.

3. **A** After the success of the inaugural Bexington Food and Music Festival last year, the event is making a return on August 16th this year.

4. **B** Our Arts by the Ocean Festival extends Bridmouth's popular summer season into an extended summer of arts.

5. **D** The complete programme is already available on the website.

6. **C** selection is by picking names from a hat for Regular Venues

7. **A** While the musical line-up is yet to be confirmed

8. **tenants** This service lets tenants pay their rent or council tax in nominated Post Office branches using cards or cash.

9. **stamps** Local authorities can sell stamps for these essential services at selected Post Office branches. People simply pop in branch and buy them to show they've bought a Home Care service

10. **vouchers** Customers can pop into a branch and purchase vouchers in order to pay for this service.

11. **procedures** People can conduct their application, enrolment and identification procedures in order to renew their Photocard Driving Licence for 10 years.

12. **error rates** Error rates with this service offered at our branches are consistently between 1% and 2%, compared to over 10% for applications sent direct to the Identity and Passport Service.

13. **characteristics** Their biometric information is unique characteristics that can be used to identify them.

14. **signatures** we will scan their fingers and thumbs (10 digits) and photograph their face digitally. We'll also capture a digital copy of applicants' signatures and send the application to the Border Agency for approval.

15. **scope** Priorities and project plans will change, deadlines will be missed, scope will be expanded, but communication must stay consistent.

16. **cumulative effect** First, create the 'critical path', which is the tasks that need to be done and their particular order. These are the places where projects can get behind and where the cumulative effect is not meeting the project target.

17. **praise** And don't save praise only for the times when things are going well - it's almost more important to boost morale through recognising hard work and effort when things don't go as planned - as things don't often go as planned!

18. **obstacles** One of the most important things a project manager can do is to eliminate obstacles for their teams. That can help keep projects within the agreed-upon framework, make the workflow more efficient and keep everything on schedule.

19. **talents** To be a better project manager, you must be intimately familiar with each team member. Familiarise yourself with the unique talents of each person on his team so you know who would and who wouldn't be good for particular jobs. By doing so, you can better predict what challenges may arise and how to overcome them.

20. **protocols** You can also adopt protocols to help keep those chronically late team members on track by building in additional time for approvals.

21. **YES** But there are many other issues to consider, such as whether you want to do business with a particular supplier again.

22. **NO** Do not indicate that there are things you're prepared to concede or compromise on too early in the negotiations.

23. **NO** If the other party keeps referring to urgent deadlines or a person they need to confer with, remember they may be using pressure tactics. Use such strategies yourself with caution, as they can be very irritating.

24. **NOT GIVEN** There is nothing in the text relating to this and so the answer is 'not given' in the text.

25. **YES** If the current state of the supplier's market means prices are falling, point this out, as their profit margins will be higher and they'll be able to offer you a better deal.

26. **NOT GIVEN** There is nothing in the text relating to this and so the answer is 'not given' in the text.

27. **NO** Even if you are a supplier's main customer and enjoy most of the bargaining power, forcing it to meet prices at which it could go out of business won't protect your reputation as a highly valued customer. The supplier will soon look for other customers and is likely to feel resentful.

28. **A plywood framework** When we build a wall with concrete today, a plywood framework is constructed, concrete is poured into it, and when the concrete is cured, it is removed, leaving the concrete wall.

29. **Mortar** In ancient Rome, two freestanding, parallel walls were built of brick bound with mortar, the combination of which is much, much stronger than plywood.

30. **A cavity** A cavity a couple feet wide was left between the brick walls, and then concrete was poured in, along with some small rocks to bolster stability.

31. **FALSE**   A most unusual Roman structure depicting their technical advancement is the Pantheon. This is a brick faced building constructed to praise the Roman gods

32. **FALSE**   In the centre of the dome is a 19-foot opening held in place by a bronze ring backed by a brick ring integrated into the concrete dome. This ingenious opening admitted sunlight to brighten the interior and the slightly curved marble floor provided drainage.

33. **NOT GIVEN**   There is nothing in the text relating to this and so the answer is 'not given' in the text.

34. **TRUE**   To protect the surfaces of the clay from erosion, the ancients discovered that a coating of thin, white, burnt limestone would chemically combine with the gases in the air to give a hard protecting and moisture proof shield.

35. **TRUE**   Later, it was found that mixing a little volcanic ash in a fine powder with the moist lime not only made a thicker coat for the ancient concrete, but also produced a durable product that could be submerged in water

36. **TRUE**   Roller compacted concrete consists of a mixture of 40 per cent Portland cement and 60 percent fly ash, a byproduct of electric power plants.

37. **B***   A new concrete product called roller compacted concrete was developed in the last century and this concrete mimics some of ancient concrete's characteristics. Roller compacted concrete consists of a mixture of 40 per cent Portland cement and 60 percent fly ash, a byproduct of electric power plants. By coincidence, the fly ash contains the same amorphous silica compounds as the ash from explosive volcanoes, and, when mixed, the hydrated Portland cement releases the calcium component recognised in the lime mixing part of the ancient concrete formula.

38. **D***   By coincidence, the fly ash contains the same amorphous silica compounds as the ash from explosive volcanoes, and, when mixed, the hydrated Portland cement releases the same calcium component recognised in the lime mixing part of the ancient concrete formula

39. **E***   Again, we have a similarity in the ancient and roller compacted concrete practices, which is little water used and tightly compacting the materials in their placement.

40. **G***   The materials (and their ratios) are very similar in both ancient and modern roller compacted concrete and the technique of tamping stiff mortar into the voids of a rock layer to avoid empty spaces are also common to both.

EXAMPLE WRITING ANSWERS

Below you will find example writing answers for all the writing questions in the General Practice Tests 21 to 25. There are many ways of answering the writing questions and these examples are only one possibility of a good answer. Please refer to the question papers while you are reading these letters and essays so that you understand the questions that are being answered. We hope this will give you an insight into how the writing answers should be written for IELTS General module.

GENERAL WRITING PRACTICE TEST 21

Task 1

Dear Madam,

My name is Patricia Wilson and I had the pleasure of attending the lecture you organised earlier this week on the reducing bee population. I cannot tell you how much I enjoyed the lecture. The gentleman who gave it was knowledgeable and interesting and had the ability to pass on his information in a fascinating and interactive way.

I was hoping that it would be possible for me to contact the lecturer in order that I could show my appreciation. I realise that you might not be able to pass on his contact details and, in that case, would you pass on my address so that he may contact me? I also have an opportunity for him to deliver the same lecture at a society that I am a member of.

I know that you organise regular lectures and I hope you don't mind if I suggest a topic that you might be able to find someone to talk about. The reducing bee population is a very important issue and, similarly, the butterfly population is also getting smaller. Might it be possible that someone could talk about this?

Thank you again for organising such a wonderful evening!

Yours sincerely,

Patricia Wilson

(203 words)

Task 2

It indeed appears true that the frequency with which advertisements for charities appear both on television and the Internet seems to be increasing. There can be various explanations for this and it can be seen in both a positive and negative light.

One explanation for the increase in the number of charity advertisements is that the charities themselves are becoming more aggressive in their marketing. This can also be seen in the common strategy nowadays to encourage a monthly donation, rather than a one-off donation. The increased marketing is apparent too in the increased numbers of 'street salespeople', who stop passersby and try to get them to commit to this monthly payment.

A second reason for the increase could also be that there have been more charities started and the number of advertisements would therefore increase and become more noticeable. If these charities are all legitimate, this would mean that more help will be getting to causes that need it. The increase in charities could also be explained by a possible increase of humanitarian awareness. People might be now adopting different ideologies that take into account people in less advantageous positions.

If the number of advertisements for charities has risen due to the fact that there has been a positive shift in people's compassionate principles, this surely has to be seen as an optimistic development. If it is due to the fact that governments have been cutting back, it could be seen as a pessimistic development. In addition, if there are more charities asking for more money, this will inevitably mean that the amount of money donated will have to be more thinly spread, which would be a negative development.

There could be several reasons for why there are more charity advertisements today. Whatever the reasons, as long as any money is helping people in disadvantageous positions, it must be seen as a positive development.

(315 words)

GENERAL WRITING PRACTICE TEST 22

Task 1

Dear John,

This is Gary. I'm sorry to have to write to you, but I seem to have lost your phone number and email address!

As you may remember, when I saw you last month, you lent me your electric lawn mower. Thank you so much for this. I have finally got around to mowing my lawn and it did a fantastic job.

Unfortunately, when I had finished cutting the grass, I was wheeling your mower back to my shed while it was still running and I cut through the electric cable. I had a look at the cable and, in my opinion, it cannot be fixed. I am so sorry.

I will take the lawn mower to the dealer in town on Saturday and try and get a replacement cable for the mower. I am confident this will be possible, but, if it isn't, I will buy you a replacement mower and bring it round to your house in the afternoon.

Once again, I'm really very sorry to have damaged the cable, but I hope to have the problem fixed by the end of this Saturday.

All the best,

Gary

(192 words)

Task 2

It has been a popular trend for some time now to put children into what can be called 'work experience placements'. The children are taken out of school and take part in various types of work, usually for around a week. Some people criticise this trend, but I can't see how it can be a negative experience.

One of the criticisms is that children lose a week of schoolwork. With the pressure to do well at school increasing, children need every bit of help to maximise their potential. Taking them out of the school, it is therefore argued, stops them from getting access to needed education for a whole week. As the children won't really be of much help to a workplace for just one week, it would therefore be better for them to remain at school.

While this is a valid point, taking a child's entire experience of school into account, a single week away does not make a significant difference. Indeed, if the timing of the week's work placements is done correctly, the week can also serve as a kind of 'holiday' away from school, something that is regularly needed in order to allow children to remain fresh and enthusiastic. In many work placements, children also get to see some of things they learn at school put into a realistic context, allowing the children to understand the relevance of what they learn and thereby creating a way to reinforce the learning.

In addition to this, children can be quite nervous about the world of work that they will have to join at some point in their lives. By getting this short taste of what it is like, they can see that it is nothing to be scared about. As well as this, children will often have some ideas of what they want to do for a living, but are not sure. By allowing them to see a type of work they are considering, they are better able to decide whether that career could be suitable for them.

I feel, therefore, that work placements can be seen as a positive development. Missing a short amount of school is not serious and the benefits that can be gained from the placements are significant. *(373 words)*

GENERAL WRITING PRACTICE TEST 23

Task 1

Dear Mrs. Johnson,

This is Robert Powell, your sales account executive on the second floor.

As you know, I've been doing some work that has involved the installation of new software on my work computer. The software is excellent and it allows me to complete my tasks much more efficiently.

Unfortunately, the new software has slowed down my computer to an unacceptable level. Every morning, it takes at least half an hour to boot up correctly and during the day, there are several times when it freezes and I need to restart the computer, which means waiting for it again. This significantly affects my productivity.

Yesterday evening, I visited an IT shop. They told me that I can increase the RAM and get a service, which should speed up my computer significantly. This will cost around 100 dollars. If this does not work, I will need to have a new computer. The current brand I have with the required software installed would cost 800 dollars. My opinion is that we should try and get my computer upgraded first and, based on the success or failure of that, make the decision regarding a new one. I can do this as soon as you give me permission to proceed.

Yours sincerely,

Robert Powell   *(211 words)*

Task 2

With the rise of cheaper airlines and with technology and affluence allowing people to travel more easily, tourism is an industry that has experienced a significant increase. This caused the numbers of tourists in some popular cities to become greater than desirable and created some effects on both individuals and society.

One positive effect of this phenomenon for both individuals and society is that it is an indicator that people are travelling to different countries. In my opinion, travel is a great way to broaden the mind and develop more understanding and acceptance of other cultures and beliefs. Individuals will become more tolerant and society should be more integrated and peaceful. Another positive effect is that jobs and businesses are created and supported by the tourism industry, thus generating taxes to help support government infrastructures.

There are negative effects though, especially for the inhabitants of the cities with high numbers of tourists. It is well known that excessive tourism dilutes the authentic culture of the destination and prices go up and the quality of products and services go down. The historic centres of too many popular cities now seem to only feature the same chain stores and services, and food tends to become more internationalised rather than offering the authentic food of the country and region.

Accommodation is another area where negative effects can be seen. The centres of very busy tourist towns become overly geared towards providing accommodation for rent, whether it is hotels, hostels or private apartments. This reduces the amount of housing for locals, as well as driving up rental and purchase prices. The locals often will move away from the centre of the city, thereby making the destination even less of an authentic representation of the country that the tourists have come to see. There have been many recent demonstrations against this situation in towns such as Barcelona and Venice, and the Italian island of Capri.

Tourism has many positive effects, but when the numbers of tourists get so high, it can spoil the authenticity of a destination, which is negative for local and visiting individuals and society as a whole.   *(355 words)*

GENERAL WRITING PRACTICE TEST 24

Task 1

Dear Sir / Madam,

My name is Cara Smith. Yesterday I had lunch at your restaurant. Unfortunately, I left my mobile phone at my table.

When I arrived at your restaurant, I was shown to table 5, by the window. I saw my phone was nearly out of battery, so I asked my waiter if I could recharge it from one of your sockets and he graciously said that was fine. I plugged my phone in in a socket behind the curtain next to the window. As my phone was out of sight, I forgot to pick it up when I left. Because it is behind the curtain, it's probably still there. I've tried calling it, but I know that I had it on silent, so no one has heard it.

My phone is a brushed aluminium Samsung smart phone. It is fairly large, as I do a lot of business writing on it. The screen saver is a picture of my daughter, who is three years old with long blond hair.

If possible, I think the best thing is that you just put my phone into a drawer and I will come by the restaurant at the end of the week when I'm in your town again to pick it up. This will save you having to do anything extra.

I look forward to seeing you again at the end of the week.

Yours sincerely,

Cara Smith

(238 words)

Task 2

It is indeed true that digital resources today far outstrip what can be put and stored in print books. Almost any kind of book can now be accessed digitally and those that can't be will soon be changed to a digital format. Some people therefore believe that libraries with print books are no longer needed.

If one looks at this issue dispassionately, it seems far more logical that people now should only read books digitally. It only requires a single computer or electronic reader and an individual can have access to the history of literature and works on all other fields. The costs involved with setting, typing, printing and distributing print books would practically disappear and this would make things more convenient and much cheaper. An actual library building would be totally unnecessary, as all one would need would be a 'virtual library' as a website and all works could be accessed through this portal. There would not even be any need to leave the house to gain access to anything one needed. This would seem to be the most logical way of proceeding.

Logic, however, is not always the best approach to everything. Print books have a long history with humanity and our relationship with real books is not something that can be changed overnight. Many people, including younger readers, feel that there is something special about having a book with real paper and needing to turn pages. There will therefore for the time being be a future for print books and libraries.

Libraries will continue to be especially important, as not all older people use computers and e-readers as much as the younger generation. They will still want to read print books and the library is a cheap and convenient place to find them. In addition, if only a few books in print are available in the future, libraries might be one of the few places where they might be accessed. Another purpose that libraries serve is acting as community centres that organise events, education and childcare. Ironically, libraries also provide computers and Internet access for people who cannot afford their own.

In spite of the seeming dominance to come of digital books, I feel that there is and will be a place for libraries with print books. This state of affairs might change in the future, but at present, they are important community resources.

(397 words)

GENERAL WRITING PRACTICE TEST 25

Task 1

Dear Jane,

This is Mary from next door. I hope you're well and enjoying life. I don't know if you knew, but I'm on holiday in Spain. I'm really enjoying some relaxation time; the weather is good and I'm spending plenty of time on the beach.

I'm writing to ask you for a favour. Next Monday (the 25th) at 9 a.m., I have arranged to have a package with some books delivered to my house. I had totally forgotten that I had planned to go on holiday. I really don't want to miss the delivery, so I was wondering if you might be able to wait by my front door for the delivery. The company is usually very punctual and you wouldn't have to wait for long. If you can do this, send me a text on 527 463 812 and I'll let the company know that you will be there.

I will be coming back at lunchtime on the following Wednesday (the 28th). I know that you'll be at work then, so I'll come round in the evening to pick up the package.

I hope you'll be able to do this, as I can't think of anyone else I can trust.

Best wishes,

Mary

(205 words)

Task 2

If one wants to work for money, there are really only two options, working for someone else for a salary and being self-employed. Most people are involved with these two options and they both have advantages and disadvantages.

Being self-employed means that the worker owns the business that is being done. This might be a small one-person business or a large company with hundreds of employees. The first advantage of this is the capacity to earn more money. If the business does very well, the income can be considerable and the owner of the company will receive the benefits. On the other hand, if business is not good, the owner's income will be low. Self-employed people also have the benefit to some extent of choosing their working hours and holidays and they have the right to change anything within their business. With this autonomy, however, comes the pressure to succeed and the reliance on one's employees, if there are any, to do their best to make the business thrive.

Salaried workers do not experience the same stress as the self-employed owners of companies. They might have stress in their duties, but the pressure that comes with keeping one's own business operating successfully in order to support oneself and one's family is just not felt by an employee. The employee also has a certain knowledge of his or her income, as the salary is usually fixed every month. The self-employed owner's income often depends on how successful the business is. The employee's fixed income, however, does not give much scope for earning large amounts more. In addition, an employee does not have the freedoms of the owner or the autonomy, and for many people, having control over their lives is a significant factor to their well-being.

It is certain that there are advantages and disadvantages for both being self-employed and salaried. I personally disagree that being salaried is better than being self-employed. I prefer the autonomy that being self-employed brings and, although there is more risk and pressure, this can lead to greater and more fulfilling rewards.

(346 words)

COMMENTARY ON THE EXAMPLE SPEAKING RECORDINGS

In this section you will find reports by an IELTS speaking examiner on the recordings of **Speaking Tests 21 - 25**. The questions asked in the recordings are the questions in the Speaking Tests 21 – 25, so, while listening to the recordings, it is advised to have the questions with you for reference. The recordings are not real IELTS test recordings, but the interviewer is a real IELTS examiner and the recordings are conducted in the exact way that an IELTS Speaking Test is done.

SPEAKING PRACTICE TEST 21

Examiner's Commentary

The person interviewed is Vishvak, an Indian male. Vishvak is a scientist.

Part 1

Vishvak gave a very good Part 1. He was very fluent and his speeches were consistently coherent and accomplished. Vishvak clearly had a wide range of lexis at his disposal and nearly always showed appropriate and natural vocabulary choices. Examples included "go for", "curd rice", "localised", "accessible", "densely populated", "concrete jungles" and "social web". Vishvak's grammatical range and accuracy was also excellent, with no real errors made. Vishvak spoke with a very slight Indian accent, but this did not affect his communicative ability in any way.

Part 2

Vishvak's Part 2 showed again that he had a very good command of English. He spoke for around 1 minute, 25 seconds, but his communication was a little fragmentary, which stopped him showing the fluency that he showed in Part 1. Vishvak's lexical resource was fine, but he was not able to produce many complex lexis, though the lexis that he used were used accurately and appropriately. Vishvak's grammar was also accurate, though limited in scope. What he used was fine, but more developed sentences would have allowed him to show more complex grammatical and syntactic structures. Again, Vishvak's pronunciation was clear. He was able to use tone and stress reasonably well, but again the somewhat fragmentary nature of his speeches limited him.

Part 3

The more demanding questions were handled well by Vishvak. He spoke fluently and coherently, though I felt he could have provided fuller answers, giving me a better picture of his English abilities. Vishvak's answers were a little hesitant from time to time as he considered his answers, but the way Vishvak spoke was not materially different to when he answered the questions in Part 1. Vishvak again showed he had the lexical resources to deal with any of the questions asked him. Some vocabulary items that stood out were "petting", "soothing", "poaching", "toxins", "biodegradable", "confines" and "demographic". There was an interesting moment when he tried to experiment with creating the verb "deincentivise", but he didn't quite form the word correctly. Again, Vishvak's grammar usage was accurate and reasonably varied. As through the rest of the speaking test, verbs were correctly formed, verb patterns were correct and syntax was wholly appropriate. Vishvak's pronunciation was again very good. He was able to skillfully use tone, stress and intonation to add meaning to what he said.

Marking - The marking of the IELTS Speaking Test is done in 4 parts.

Fluency and Coherence	8
Lexical Resource	8.5
Grammatical Range and Accuracy	8.5
Pronunciation	9
Estimated IELTS Speaking Band	**8.5**

SPEAKING PRACTICE TEST 22

Examiner's Commentary

The person interviewed is Grace, a Taiwanese female. Grace is a teacher.

Part 1

Grace spoke fluently and clearly. She was often a little hesitant in giving answers, but this seemed to be from considering answers, rather than a lack of language to deal with the questions. Grace also seemed to be happy with merely giving a "yes" or "no" answer and needed a "why" to expand. I feel it's better if candidates are able to produce longer response without being prompted. Grace had excellent lexical resources, using expressions and lexis such as "good at being good", "memorise", "excel", "umbrella" used metaphorically, "road rage", "frustrating", "developed/developing countries", "traffic flow", "detail" and "benign". There were occasional inconsistencies in word choice, such as "I'm somewhat of a pessimistic", but this did not affect communication. Grace's grammatical range and accuracy was excellent and she used a variety of complex structures such as a second conditional, ("if they were to be made legal") and a continuous passive, ("currently being debated). Again, there were a few minor errors, such as "in the past they don't drive very well". Grace's Taiwanese accent was clearly discernable and her Chinese mother tongue created occasional unusual stress placements and intonation, but her communicative ability was never affected.

Part 2

Although Grace spoke fluently in Part 2, she did not talk for very long. The required time for a student to speak in Part 2 is between 1 and 2 minutes and Grace spoke for only 50 seconds. Grace's vocabulary was again good and she used items such as "the back of my mind", "lap", "cigarette butt", "passed away" and "fished out". Her grammatical range and accuracy was also good, but not without error. She said "it's really coming from", which was an awkward use of the continuous, "I recently digged out" instead of using the correct irregular past "dug" and "I have not got a chance to talk to him", which should have been "I did not have", as the uncle referred to is deceased. Grace's accent was always noticeable and there was some minor awkwardness with stress and intonation, but communication was not affected in any way.

Part 3

Grace spoke fluently and coherently in Part 3. She was a little slow at the start, but this was more to access ideas rather than language. Grace's ideas were built well on each other and she was able to use discourse markers (such as "let's see" and "but then again") to direct her speech. Grace's lexical resource was again excellent. There were no real awkward choices and plenty of more complex items, such as, "procrastinate", "reinforce", "subconsciously", "reserved", "means", "stimulus" and "focused". Grace's grammar range and accuracy were again very accurate in Part 3. There were no real errors and also she employed some more complex structures, for example the use of the 'future in the past': "what would I look like". Grace's speech in Part 3 was still accented but very clear, and communication was rarely affected. She is able to use tone and intonation to add meaning and she likes to vary the pace of her speech delivery to good effect.

Marking - The marking of the IELTS Speaking Test is done in 4 parts.

Fluency and Coherence	7.5
Lexical Resource	8.5
Grammatical Range and Accuracy	7.5
Pronunciation	8
Estimated IELTS Speaking Band	**8**

SPEAKING PRACTICE TEST 23

Examiner's Commentary

The person interviewed is Alexander, a Kazakh male. Alexander is a student.

Part 1

Alexander showed in Part 1 that he had a good command of English. He spoke clearly and fluently, but he nearly always gave very short answers and some answers were a little stilted. This detracted from his overall performance, as he did not appear as fluent as he probably could have been and it would have been better if Alexander had been able to show off a bit more with longer answers. In the end, Part 1 was only around three and a quarter minutes. In spite of the limited amount of language produced, Alexander showed he had a very good lexical range. He usually used an appropriate word choice and produced plenty of more complex vocabulary, such as "avid", "mediocre", "reliable", "punctual", "from time to time", "dehydrated", "fully hydrated", "wells" and "in the back of my mind". Occasionally, there were some awkward choices, such as "average entertainment", "between 11 and 12 in the afternoon" instead of "in the evening", "it's very alright" and "it's very important to your health" instead of "very important for your health". Alexander showed he had excellent grammatical accuracy, though his shortish answers did not allow him to use many more complex structures. There was maybe one awkward choice when he said "frequent travels", travel being a verb or uncountable noun. Alexander spoke very clearly and all his utterances were easy to understand. There was a very minimal accent that never impeded communication. Tone could sometimes have been better used, but he also managed to give a deadpan delivery, which, with his understatement, allowed some irony and humour to come through.

Part 2

Alexander's Part 2 was quite accomplished, but he was again quite clipped and abrupt. Sentences did not flow, although he didn't seem to be pausing to access language or structures. Alexander again also spoke for too short a time. Candidates should speak for a minimum of a minute and Alexander only managed around forty-three seconds. Alexander's lexical resource was again very good with such items as "traditional", "not to my taste" and "ritual". There was only one real slip, which was when he said that "the eyeballs of the sheep are for extinguished individuals" instead of "distinguished individuals". The shortness of his Part 2 did not really allow him to show off what more he could have produced. How Alexander showed his grammatical range and accuracy had the same problem. Some nice structures were produced, for example how he used "I have been a part of", but the shortness of Part 2 did not allow him to produce a variety of structure. Alexander's pronunciation was again very good, with the slight accent not affecting comprehension in any way.

Part 3

Alexander's longer speeches in Part 3 much better showed his fluency and his ability to make coherent developed points. Although he did speak for longer, he still only barely fulfilled the minimum, so fuller answers would still have been preferable. Any minor pauses that Alexander made were really to process how he would develop his content rather than showing a difficulty in accessing vocabulary or structure. The more complex questions and Alexander speaking for a bit longer allowed a better range of lexis to be produced. There were no real poor word choices and plenty of examples of complex items, such as "supervision", "balanced", "determination", "borderline pointless", "stigma", "labelled", "protein", "building blocks", "endanger", "well-being", "prevalence", "organs", "substitution", "tactics for manipulation", "vitamins, minerals, fibres" and "engrained". In terms of grammatical range and accuracy, there were mostly fairly simple structures produced, but everything was extremely accurate and Alexander never seemed to have the need for more complex structures. Finally, Alexander was again perfectly clear in his pronunciation and any minor residual accent did not affect comprehension. It was effortless to understand him.

Marking - The marking of the IELTS Speaking Test is done in 4 parts.

Fluency and Coherence	8
Lexical Resource	8
Grammatical Range and Accuracy	8
Pronunciation	9
Estimated IELTS Speaking Band	**8**

SPEAKING PRACTICE TEST 24

Examiner's Commentary

The person interviewed is Joaquin, an Argentinian male. Joaquin is a student.

Part 1

Joaquin spoke reasonably fluently and coherently. Occasionally he stopped to think about what he needed to say next and occasionally the coherence broke down, especially at the end of sentences. This seemed to due to a lack of confidence, and nervousness. Joaquin showed an excellent lexical resource. He never really chose an inappropriate item and there were many higher level words and phrases, including "cottage-like", "encouraged and persevere", "encompasses our society", "sustainable", "on the brink" and "deforestation". Joaquin's grammatical range and accuracy was also excellent. Verb forms were accurate and there were no errors or unsuitable structures. Joaquin's pronunciation was very good. There was a slight accent, but this did not affect intelligibility in any way.

Part 2

Joaquin was more fluent in Part 2. It seemed that without the different questions, he was able to focus on developing his points and he was able to do so with good coherence. He could have spoken for a bit longer – he only managed just over a minute and maybe speaking longer would have given him the opportunity to show more of his command of English. Joaquin's lexis use was accurate and appropriate, although there weren't really any vocabulary items that stood out. Joaquin's grammatical accuracy was very good. He was describing a past event and his past tenses were accurate and well controlled. There was not a great range shown, but he didn't really need structure outside what he used. Again, Joaquin's pronunciation was excellent and he used tone, pauses and intonation to good effect.

Part 3

Joaquin was again fluent and coherent. He sometimes was a little bit hesitant in getting his sentences finished, but it was an improvement on Part 1. Joaquin's lexical resource in Part 3 was excellent. There were no real inappropriate choices and he showed a good range of well-used complex items, such as "mishandled", "profit-oriented", "means", "the stepping stone" and "mundane". Joaquin's grammar usage was highly accurate and his range of structures was always appropriate. His pronunciation was again very clear and understanding him was effortless. Tone, pauses and intonation were again skillfully used to very good effect.

Marking - The marking of the IELTS Speaking Test is done in 4 parts.

Fluency and Coherence	8
Lexical Resource	8.5
Grammatical Range and Accuracy	8.5
Pronunciation	9
Estimated IELTS Speaking Band	**8.5**

SPEAKING PRACTICE TEST 25

Examiner's Commentary

The person interviewed is Marcos, a Spanish male. Marcos is a teacher.

Part 1

Marcos spoke reasonably fluently at times, but at others he was a bit stilted and fragmentary. This also affected his coherence, as he would regularly start a sentence and then stop and begin again. Sentences were also not always clearly expressed to their ends. Marcos lexical resource was reasonable. He was able to explain most things that he wanted to, although this sometimes involved backtracking to restate ideas and paraphrase. There were some higher level items, such as "curriculum", "mentality", "open-minded" and "aware", but there were also some awkward choices, such as "Spaniard childhood" instead of "Spanish childhood", "joining the playground", "recorded in my mind", "no problem on it" and "an ignorant". Marcos' basic grammatical structures were usually accurate and some slightly more complex structures were used, such as "it's much easier". There were also, however, regular errors, such as "long time ago" instead of "a long time ago", "we play" instead of "we played" and "we are belong" instead of "we belong". Marcos spoke English with a fairly strong Spanish accent. Most of the time, his English was reasonably clear, but there were regular instances when a word was difficult to identify (for example, "naughty"). Marcos was able to use a variety of features, such as tone, stress and intonation to add meaning to his speeches.

Part 2

Marcos spoke fairly fluently and coherently, though he sometimes had to stop and restart a sentence. He spoke for around 1 minute, 15 seconds, so he easily passed the minimum requirement, but he could have spoken a little longer. Marcos showed he had the lexical resource to say whatever he wanted and good examples of his vocabulary are "doubts", "even when", "role model" and "to catch up". There were few awkward moments in terms of lexis. Marcos' grammatical range and accuracy in Part 3 were not as accomplished as Part 1. Although he produced lots of accurate structures, for example, "it has always been connected with" and "they are older than me", there were also plenty of errors or awkward structures, such as, "we growed up", "they have been always living" (word order), "they were feeding me" ("would feed" would have been better), "even though I was eating in my school" (I had eaten" would have been better), "I always repeat in their house", "three per years" and "only during Christmas or during the summer we are able to meet" (instead of "only during Christmas or during the summer are we able to meet". Marcos again spoke with a marked Spanish accent and this did affect communication sometimes. Tone, stress and intonation were again used to good effect.

Part 3

Marcos spoke reasonably fluently in Part 3, giving full answers. The more complex questions, however, created some problems, and he would sometimes construct some sentences awkwardly (for example, "that connects something with the beginning") and have to pause to search for the right language. Generally, Marcos' lexical resource was quite good and he usually had the language to deal with the questions, including some more complex items, such as, "get on very well", "you are not set in a place", "solidarity", "people, they are more focused on themselves" and "on the other hand". There were, however, also some awkward choices, such as, "it's a huge different" and "mentally sickness". Similar to Part 2, there was a mix of accurate and inaccurate grammatical structures. Most structures were well controlled, for example the superlative "the strongest relationship", but there were several errors, such as, "we are catch up very quickly" (instead of "catch up"), "we make the same stupid things" (instead of "we do the same"), "being online and find a relationship online" (instead of "being online and finding a relationship online") and "where they meet" (instead of "where they met"). Marcos' accent was again quite intrusive and it occasionally had an effect on intelligibility. On the other hand, Marcos was able to use intonation, stress and tone to add meaning to what he had to say.

Marking - The marking of the IELTS Speaking Test is done in 4 parts.

Fluency and Coherence	7
Lexical Resource	7
Grammatical Range and Accuracy	7
Pronunciation	6.5
Estimated IELTS Speaking Band	**7**

Listening Recordings' Transcripts

IELTS 5 Practice Tests, General Set 5 — LISTENING TRANSCRIPTS

LISTENING TEST 21 TRANSCRIPT

This recording is copyright.

IELTS-Blog.com listening practice tests. Test twenty-one. In the IELTS test you hear some recordings and you have to answer questions on them. You have time to read the instructions and questions and check your work. All recordings are played only once. The test is in four sections. Now turn to section one.

Section one. You will hear a conversation between a man and a woman discussing a repair to a car in a garage.

First you have some time to look at questions one to five.

(20-second gap)

Now the full test will begin. You should answer the questions as you listen, as the recording is not played twice. Listen carefully to the conversation and answer questions one to five.

Receptionist	Good morning. Welcome to Gresham Garage. How can we help you today?
Mr. Clarke	Hello. My name is Clarke. I have a problem with my car and I'd like someone to have a look at it.
Receptionist	Of course. Can I ask what kind of car it is?
Mr. Clarke	It's a Toyota.
Receptionist	Oh, we specialise in them.
Mr. Clarke	I know. That's why I came.
Receptionist	Now, can I take some details first?
Mr. Clarke	Of course.
Receptionist	Can I have your full name?
Mr. Clarke	<u>Stuart</u> Clarke. That's Stuart spelled S - T - U - A - R - T and Clarke with an E. That's C - L - A - R - K - E.
Receptionist	And what's your address?
Mr. Clarke	18 Green Lane, Cranford.
Receptionist	And the postcode?
Mr. Clarke	CR8 <u>6FR</u>.
Receptionist	Can I take a telephone number?
Mr. Clarke	I'll give you my mobile number, as you're more likely to catch me on that. It's 07538 <u>645</u> 983.
Receptionist	How would you like to pay for your bill?

Mr. Clarke	<u>Cash</u>, please.
Receptionist	Fine. Now, what seems to be the problem with the car?
Mr. Clarke	It's the <u>brakes</u>, I think. When I drove to work this morning, I felt that they were slipping a bit when I slowed down.
Receptionist	Well, I'm sure we can do something about that.

Before the conversation continues, you have some time to look at questions six to ten.

(20-second gap)

Now listen carefully and answer questions six to ten.

Receptionist	Now, can you leave the car with us today?
Mr. Clarke	That won't be a problem if I can get a taxi to get me home.
Receptionist	We can call you one without a problem. By the way, when was the last time you had your car serviced?
Mr. Clarke	It was about <u>seven</u> months ago. In February.
Receptionist	You really should have your car serviced now. As we're an accredited service station for Toyota and specialise in them, we can do a good job for you.
Mr. Clarke	I suppose that's a good idea. I don't have my <u>log book</u> with me today, though.
Receptionist	That's OK. Just bring it with you when you come to pick up the car and we'll fill it in and stamp it for you.
Mr. Clarke	That's great. When can I pick up the car?
Receptionist	We should be able to look at it later today. It should be ready tomorrow, but to be sure we'd better make it the day after tomorrow. That's <u>Wednesday</u> the twenty-sixth.
Mr. Clarke	That'll be fine. If I can't come, my wife will be able to. By the way, how much do you charge for the service?
Receptionist	We charge <u>two hundred</u> pounds for a service plus parts. As a bonus for you, we'll do the work you came in for as part of the service. Of course, we'll give you a ring if there's a problem or if we need your go ahead for any unexpected or costly work.
Mr. Clarke	Is that all?
Receptionist	Can I ask how you found out about us?
Mr. Clarke	I was meeting some friends in town and, <u>while I was waiting, I saw your advertisement in the local paper.</u> I checked you online after that and saw that you had good reviews.
Receptionist	Thank you.

That is the end of section one. You will now have half a minute to check your answers.

(30-second gap)

Now turn to section two.

Section two. You will hear a woman presenting an information talk at a hospital. First you have some time to look at questions eleven to fifteen.

(20-second gap)

Now listen carefully to the information talk and answer questions eleven to fifteen.

Hello everyone and welcome to this information evening at our hospital. This evening is mainly aimed at <u>patients</u>, but it will also be useful for their friends and families.

Your admission to hospital will depend on the type of procedure or care you will be receiving. You can attend as an outpatient, or be admitted as a day patient or an inpatient. As an outpatient, you will go to hospital for an appointment to see a specialist, but you will not stay overnight. A day patient is admitted into the hospital, but also does not stay overnight. An inpatient is admitted into the hospital and stays overnight.

If you are due to go to hospital for pre-arranged care, you will usually receive an admission letter beforehand. This will tell you the date of your admittance to hospital, which ward you are going to be in, and the consultant who will be taking care of you. <u>The admission letter</u> will also give you a contact number for your ward and will contain any special instructions you need to follow before your hospital procedure. For example, you may be asked not to eat or drink for a certain period of time before attending hospital. One thing to note is that it may be necessary for you to contact the hospital on the morning of your admission date to ensure that a bed is available for you. Sometimes, <u>emergencies</u> mean hospital beds are not available when scheduled. If a bed is not available, your admission date will be rearranged. If a bed is available, you will normally be asked to arrive at the hospital in the mid or late afternoon.

At our hospital, you will be asked to take part in a pre-admissions assessment. This may be an appointment with a nurse or doctor, but it is usually done <u>by telephone</u> to save time and money for everyone. You will be asked questions about your health, your medical history and your home circumstances. You will also be given advice about your admission, including where to report on arrival. As I said before, it's very important to realise that you may be asked not to eat or drink before coming into hospital for your tests or operation. Finally, you will also be given advice about when to take <u>medication</u> if you have any prescribed. You should always bring this to the hospital with you and give it to the nurses when you arrive, even if you have stopped taking it.

You now have some time to look at questions sixteen to twenty.

(20-second gap)

Now listen to the rest of the information talk and answer questions sixteen to twenty.

Now I'd like to let you know about what patients should bring with them when they come here for their procedure. Think of it as being at home and stuck in bed. You'll need a dressing gown and slippers for when you get out of bed. <u>Don't bring pyjamas or anything though, as all patients in the hospital have to wear our nightgowns.</u> These allow patients to be easily examined by doctors. Bring all your teeth care equipment, such as floss, brush, toothpaste and mouth wash. You should also bring a face flannel if you have one, but don't worry about towels as we supply all those. If you have to stay for any period of time at the hospital, you should ask a friend or family member to bring fresh things and take away the dirty things to launder.

Now, as you'll be staying quite a long time in bed, it's good to bring some things to help time pass. Books are a good idea and these can sometimes help send you to sleep as well, which is the best thing to help you heal. Many people today bring in e-books and as you'll have your own free power socket next to your bed, you'll be able to charge your mobile device when necessary. Computers, tablets and smart phones are all permitted, <u>but if you're watching or listening to any media, it is obligatory to wear headphones or earphones</u>, so that you don't disturb others around you.

When you arrive in the car park at the hospital, go into the main reception area. There are a number of corridors going off it. The first on the right is for outpatients and people should go there if they're having a procedure, but not staying overnight. The corridor next to that goes to the MRI and X-ray department and also to the <u>eye unit</u>. People should not go to any of these departments unless they have a referral or if they're being taken there directly from their ward.

The next corridor goes to the oncology department, the orthopaedics department and the renal unit. You'll see the signposting for these departments as you walk down.

The next corridor is very short and only goes to <u>the pharmacy</u>. Drugs and medicines can be bought here, and, as it's in a hospital, it has a much wider range of prescription and non-prescription drugs. Of course, if you're on a ward, the nursing staff will organise all your medication and you won't need to come here until maybe when you leave.

We're running a little short of time now, so I'll stop, as I want you to be able to ask some questions. I'll hand out some leaflets at the end and there's a map included, so don't worry if I haven't mentioned where you're going. If you experience any problems finding where to go when you get to the hospital, just go to <u>the information point</u> in the middle of the reception area and ask.

So, let's move onto the questions.

That is the end of section two. You will now have half a minute to check your answers.

(30-second gap)

Now turn to section three.

Section three. You will hear two students discussing their presentation on Lake Baikal. First you have some time to look at questions twenty-one to twenty-five.

(20-second gap)

Now listen carefully and answer questions twenty-one to twenty-five.

Sam   Hi, Alice. How are you today?

Alice   I'm good, thanks, Sam. A bit busy, but I'll be better when we get this presentation over with.

Sam   I know how you feel! Shall we get started straight away?

Alice   Yes. So, to recap, we're going to do a presentation on Lake Baikal in Russia. I'm going to start and give an introduction and then I'll give some information on the fauna there.

Sam   That's right. Then I'll take over and talk a little bit about the climate at the lake. So, did you have any success preparing for your part?

Alice   Yes. I'll run through my introduction first. You can make some notes and tell me what doesn't sound so good.

Sam   Good idea.

Alice   OK. So, here goes. Lake Baikal is the world's oldest and deepest freshwater lake. What geologists find interesting is that today's Lake Baikal shows what <u>seaboards</u> of North America, Africa and Europe looked like when they began to separate millions of years ago. Lake Baikal gives us an insight into what these areas were like at those times.

Sam   That's a good start. But shouldn't you give some of the basic dimensions first?

Alice   Yes, you're right. I've got that information in my next bit. I'll just move it up to the beginning and fit it in. I'll read that part for you now.

Sam   Good.

Alice   Lake Baikal is in <u>a rift</u>, where the continent of Asia is literally splitting apart. Continental rifts and their end products, such as the passive continental margins on the US east coast, are ubiquitous with the Earth's geological record. If Baikal's rift valley had existed millions of years ago, it would have created the beginnings of a future ocean. At six hundred kilometres long and seventy-nine kilometres wide, Lake Baikal has the largest surface area of any freshwater lake in Asia, at thirty-one thousand, seven hundred and twenty-two square kilometres. It is also the deepest lake in the world, at one thousand six hundred and forty-two metres. The bottom of the lake's water is one thousand one hundred and eighty-six metres below sea level, but below this lie <u>vast quantities of sediment</u>, placing the lake's rock floor some eight to eleven kilometres below the surface.

Sam   Yes, that's perfect. Just join those two bits together. How about the part about the fauna?

Alice   I found there's more information than I can really include, as Lake Baikal has so many different animal species. Some of them developed twenty-five million years ago and <u>seventy per cent</u> of them are found only in the Lake Baikal region, making its preservation crucial.

Sam   Maybe you could focus on one key species as an example?

Alice   There are two key things to mention, actually. The first is that Lake Baikal has one of only three freshwater seal populations in the world. The Baikal seals have a greater abundance of <u>blood</u>, which makes it possible to them to swim under the water for more than seventy minutes. They can also travel at great depths, sometimes going so far as three hundred meters under the surface. Second, some of the fish that live in Lake Baikal survive more than a mile below the surface. They are so well-adapted to these pressures that they will literally explode if brought to the surface, where the pressure is dramatically different.

| Sam | Good work on that. I think that'll be fine. |

You now have some time to look at questions twenty-six to thirty.

(20-second gap)

Now listen to the rest of the discussion and answer questions twenty-six to thirty.

Alice	So, how about your section on climate?
Sam	I think it's all fine now. I'll run through my section for you.
Alice	OK.
Sam	Although Lake Baikal is in Siberia, the climate around it is much milder in winter than in the rest of southern Siberia, due to the fact that large bodies of water retain heat longer than land. Even in the depths of winter, the average air temperature is minus twenty-one degrees Celsius compared with minimum temperatures of minus ninety degrees Celsius elsewhere in Siberia. In the summer, the temperature does not get very warm. In August, the average air temperature is nine degrees Celsius, whereas the rest of Siberia has an average of sixteen degrees Celsius. The lake freezes over from January until May or June, but its <u>average surface temperature</u> in August lies between ten and twelve degrees Celsius.
Alice	That seems like a good, basic introduction. Did you address the issue of water quality?
Sam	Yes, I did research that. Lake Baikal's water is very clear, because it lacks <u>minerals</u>. This clarity is maintained by large numbers of planktonic animals eating floating debris. In spite of its great depth, the water in the lake is well mixed, and <u>oxygen</u> is plentiful, even in the lower waters.
Alice	Where does Lake Baikal's water come from?
Sam	Half the water flowing into the lake comes down from the Selenga River in the southeast. The rest comes from more than three hundred other rivers and streams, most of which flow down from the surrounding mountains. Lake Baikal's only <u>outlet</u> is the Angara River, which flows westward from the lake's southwestern end.
Alice	Really! That's the only way water leaves the lake?
Sam	Yes. The lake doesn't even lose much water through <u>evaporation</u>, due to the comparatively low temperatures.
Alice	Is that all you have?
Sam	It is at the moment. I've got plenty of notes though and I'll finish it off tonight.
Alice	You'd better. The presentation is in two days.
Sam	I'm sorry. I've been busy on that essay we were given last week. Don't worry though. I'll have it all ready by tomorrow morning.

That is the end of section three. You will now have half a minute to check your answers.

(30-second gap)

Now turn to section four.

Section 4. You will hear part of a conservation lecture on the Siberian tiger. First you have some time to look at questions thirty-one to forty.

(50-second gap)

Now listen carefully and answer questions thirty-one to forty.

Good morning and welcome to this conservation lecture. Of all the animals we have looked at, the tiger is one of the most magnificent. The tiger has many different sub-species, but today we are going to discuss the Siberian tiger.

The Siberian tiger is the largest sub-species of tiger and is primarily found in southeastern Russia and northern China. From the 1940's to the 1960's, it was close to extinction because of hunting, with only around forty individuals left in the wild. However, its numbers recovered and, by the 1980's, there were around five hundred living in the wild. The subspecies was saved by Russia, which became the first country in the world to grant the tiger full protection, and also by the Cold War, which saw the tiger's forest home completely closed off to most people. However, at the time of the collapse of the Soviet Union, poaching and habitat destruction once again affected the Siberian tiger and numbers dropped to four hundred and fifty. Since then, continued conservation and anti-poaching efforts by many partners have helped keep the population stable at today's figure of around four hundred and fifty.

Siberian tigers were once found throughout the boreal forests in the Russian Far East, China, and the Korean peninsula. The subspecies is now restricted to certain provinces of the Russian Far East, and possibly to small pockets in the border areas of China and North Korea.

Boreal forests are temperate, with many coniferous trees such as spruce, fir, and pine. They are bordered to the north by treeless tundra and to the south by steppes. These are amongst the coldest areas in the world. The latitude means long winters, where the sun does not rise far above the horizon and the winter temperatures can drop below minus forty-five degrees Celsius in the Siberian tiger habitat. Since the typical Siberian tiger habitat is cold and the land is covered by snow during the long winters, the Siberian tiger has developed remarkably thick fur. The harsh climate in this part of the world has also made it necessary for the Siberian tiger to store excessive fat along the belly and flanks.

The most immediate threat to the survival of Siberian tigers is poaching to supply demand for tiger parts for use in traditional Chinese medicine. For more than a thousand years, the use of tiger parts has been included in the traditional Chinese medicine regimen. The Chinese culture believes that some parts of the tiger have medicinal qualities, which help cure chronic diseases and replenish the body's essential energy.

Tiger parts such as bones, eyes, whiskers and teeth are used to treat ailments and diseases ranging from insomnia and malaria, to meningitis and bad skin. Chinese texts state that the active ingredients in tiger bone can help promote healing, and that they also have anti-inflammatory properties.

Western medical experts tend to discount all claims of any curative power in tiger bone, as they do with the rhinoceros horn, another popular Chinese medicine. Also, it is well known that aspirin contains the properties believed to be in tiger products and will achieve the same supposed results.

Another significant long-term threat to Siberian tigers is habitat loss and, as a result, there is a decrease in prey. Tiger forests are at risk from logging, conversion to agriculture, urban expansion, road construction, mining, fires, and inadequate law enforcement. The latter in particular fails to deal with the problem of illegal logging, which is widespread throughout the Russian Far East. Elk, wild boar, and sika deer have also all been over-hunted by people, which in this remote area serve as a primary source of protein for humans.

Finally, one further problem Siberian tigers face is the fact that the current population is derived from just a few dozen individuals that survived the human attentions of the first half of the twentieth century. As a result, scientists fear the tigers lack sufficient genetic diversity. This means that all of today's wild Siberian tigers may be so genetically similar to one another that healthy breeding is a serious issue. Many of the Siberian tigers are now as close as siblings, or even twins, so that, amongst other problems, an illness capable of killing one of them would likely also be able to kill all of them, because of the fact that their immune systems have the same weaknesses.

So, what's being done? Wildlife conservation agencies are trying to conserve tiger populations and regional biodiversity by channelling funds to appropriate agencies to control widespread poaching of tigers and other wildlife. Russian scientists and politicians, conservationists, and local stakeholders are continually preparing and implementing habitat conservation plans to develop a comprehensive wildlife and resource management plan for the Siberian tigers' habitats. Finally, the really key element is that everyone must support educational programmes aimed at promoting habitat and conservation issues within the local communities that share the environment with the Siberian tiger.

That is the end of section four. You will now have half a minute to check your answers.

(30-second gap)

This is the end of listening test twenty-one. In the IELTS test you would now have ten minutes to transfer your answers to the listening answer sheet.

LISTENING TEST 22 TRANSCRIPT

This recording is copyright.

IELTS-Blog.com listening practice tests. Test twenty-two. In the IELTS test you hear some recordings and you have to answer questions on them. You have time to read the instructions and questions and check your work. All recordings are played only once. The test is in four sections. Now turn to section one.

Section one. You will hear a conversation between a man and a woman as the woman interviews the man about a job.

First you have some time to look at questions one to five.

(20-second gap)

Now the full test will begin. You should answer the questions as you listen, as the recording is not played twice. Listen carefully to the conversation and answer questions one to five.

Dominic	Hello. My name's Dominic. I'm here for a job interview at the beach office.
Mrs. Adams	Hello Dominic. I'm Mrs. Adams. I'm interviewing you today. Thanks for coming in.
Dominic	You're welcome. Thanks for asking me.
Mrs. Adams	Now, you've applied for the seasonal job of beach cleaner, is that right?
Dominic	Yes, that's right.
Mrs. Adams	I've had a look at your CV and it seems you're the kind of person we're after and I'm happy that you've dressed smartly, so really all I need to do is tell you a little about the job and see if you're happy with what you'll have to do. First of all though I need to take some details for the payroll office, if that's alright?
Dominic	Of course.
Mrs. Adams	To begin with, I need your full name and address.
Dominic	My name's Dominic <u>Fuller</u> and I live at 34 Queens Crescent, Stanmore. The post code's ST5 932.
Mrs. Adams	Thanks. Could you just spell Fuller for me?
Dominic	Of course. It's F – U – L – L – E – R.
Mrs. Adams	And when were you born?
Dominic	On the second September <u>nineteen ninety-eight</u>.
Mrs. Adams	Thank you. Now, have you done any work before this year?
Dominic	No. I'm a student and so this will just be my summer job.
Mrs. Adams	Now, do you know your national insurance number?

Dominic	I actually brought it with me. It's FL 63 <u>85</u> 2 H.
Mrs. Adams	Good. Do you have a P45 from a previous job?
Dominic	No. I'm afraid not. My last job was so long ago that I've lost the P45.
Mrs. Adams	That's OK. It doesn't matter. Next is your phone number. Can I have a mobile number for you that we can use?
Dominic	Yes. My number's 07535 391 2 double 8.
Mrs. Adams	Right, I've got that. Are you happy to occasionally use your phone while at work for work purposes?
Dominic	That's fine. I have <u>unlimited minutes</u> with my phone contract.
Mrs. Adams	Good. Now, how would you like to be paid?
Dominic	Actually, I would prefer <u>in cash</u>, but I don't know if that's possible.
Mrs. Adams	Yes, it is. You'll need though to come to me here at the central office every Friday after the evening shift to pick up and sign for your wages. Is that OK?
Dominic	Yes, that's fine.

Before the conversation continues, you have some time to look at questions six to ten.

(20-second gap)

Now listen carefully and answer questions six to ten.

Mrs. Adams	Now I'll tell you a little more about the job and ask a few more questions.
Dominic	Good.
Mrs. Adams	So, you'll be required to work twice a day, seven days a week. The morning shift is from <u>six</u> a.m. to nine a.m. and the evening shift is from seven p.m. to ten p.m. Do those times cause any problems for you?
Dominic	No, that should be fine. On Fridays I have a lecture that finishes at half past six, but I should be able to make work on time.
Mrs. Adams	I'll let your <u>supervisor</u> know about that in case you're delayed sometimes, but try and be on time if you can.
Dominic	It should be fine.
Mrs. Adams	As you know, the beach here is around ten kilometres and different teams start work at different locations. Do you have transport to get to the different parts of the beach?
Dominic	I've got my <u>bicycle</u>, so I'll ride to the places. I don't think the bus service goes to all the places where you might need me.
Mrs. Adams	No, it doesn't. What the job entails is to clear the sand of any rubbish in the

evening and early morning. Unfortunately, people often leave a lot of trash, whether they are lying on the beach during the day, or walking or having a party at night.

Dominic Yes, it's a shame, isn't it?

Mrs. Adams I'm afraid so. Now a lot of things you might have to pick up could be dirty or sharp. Because of this, we require that you wear <u>gloves</u> to protect yourself. We will supply these to you, as they must be worn at all times when cleaning on the beach. Do you understand that?

Dominic Yes.

Mrs. Adams Good. It affects our insurance if you don't wear them and also we want to make sure that you're safe.

Dominic I understand. It makes perfect sense anyway. I don't want to hurt myself. Is there anything else I need to wear?

Mrs. Adams Whatever you want, really. Long trousers are best and you'll need to look at the weather in order to decide. Remember the evenings can get cold, too.

Dominic OK.

Mrs. Adams You might also find <u>valuables</u> that have been lost on the beach. We ask you to hand these in when you find them, as losing things can cause a lot of distress to people. We get lots of calls to our lost property office and people are very happy when we say we've found what they've lost.

Dominic Yes, I would imagine they would be very happy!

Mrs. Adams Now, I'll just get you to sign this form to say that you confirm everything on it and then let's go outside and meet some of the crew who are working this afternoon.

That is the end of section one. You will now have half a minute to check your answers.

(30-second gap)

Now turn to section two.

Section two. You will hear a woman presenting an information talk at a museum on Australian canals. First you have some time to look at questions eleven to fourteen.

(20-second gap)

Now listen carefully to the information talk and answer questions eleven to fourteen.

Hello everyone and welcome to the Australian Museum of Canals. One frequently asked question as soon as people arrive here is, "Are there any canals in Australia?" The answer is of course, "Yes! We do have some Australian canals, but they are not suitable for cruising holidays."

After I have finished speaking, you will be free to wander around the museum and see all the exhibits. Unfortunately, <u>our café is being refurbished</u> due to a fire risk and so that is closed for a couple of weeks. There are, however, some drinks and snack machines that can be used temporarily.

Each exhibit has information given on notice boards, but there is also the chance to use the complementary guide phones, which are available at the desk next to the entrance. There is a bin next to the exit for the phones' return at the end of your visit, next to the charity box, where you can leave a few dollars if you want for the upkeep of the museum.

In ten minutes, there is a twenty-minute film shown in the small movie theatre located next to the bathrooms. This is repeated half an hour after the start of the each showing and shows a fascinating history of the development of canals in Australia. Make sure you get there a few minutes early in order to guarantee a seat for yourself.

Finally, if you have any feedback to provide us, we have now removed our feedback box that was at the exit. We've entered the twenty-first century and visitors can leave feedback on our website on a dedicated form. Please don't email, as we have too much SPAM and feedback is often lost if we're contacted in this way.

You now have some time to look at questions fifteen to twenty.

(20-second gap)

Now listen to the rest of the information talk and answer questions fifteen to twenty.

So, let me now tell you a little about some of our Australian canals. The first I'd like to mention is Berry's Canal, which was also the first canal to be established in Australia. Alexander Berry had chosen for himself some land on which to found an estate near the Hunter River. While establishing himself on the property that the government granted him, a boat carrying a friend of his was seeking a passage into the river from a tributary adjoining his property. The boat was overturned and the friend was drowned, an accident that Berry bitterly regretted. To allow vessels to travel more safely, Berry had a short canal cut between the river and the tributary, so creating a new island which, unfortunately for Berry, the government later refused to regard as part of his grant. The canal, which was one hundred and ninety-one metres long, was completed in twelve days. Later on, because of the weight of traffic on the Berry Canal, the Clarke Canal was cut, running almost parallel to the Berry. As traffic on the Berry slowly subsided, the Clarke Canal was used less and less and it was actually filled in following the Second World War, as the land was needed for other uses.

Next I'd like to talk about the four kilometre long Alexandra Canal, which is one of the main tributaries of the Cooks River, today located near the Sydney Airport. Originally it was a narrow, winding partially tidal creek into which wool washes, tanneries and chemical manufacturers discharged their effluent. Between 1887 and 1900, the creek was excavated to form the Alexandra Canal, named in honour of Princess Alexandra. It's a rare example of a nineteenth Century canal construction, being one of only two navigable channels built and still extant in New South Wales. Its construction by unemployed relief workers during the 1890's depression was an impressive achievement, taking over a decade to complete. Built in 1910, there is also an interesting subsidiary canal that joins the Alexandra Canal near the airport. This canal is known as the Cook Canal and was built to link the workshops and construction yards that serviced the traffic on the Alexandra Canal. During the excavation of the Cook Canal, dugong bones, aboriginal axes and the remains of an ancient forest below the low tide level were discovered. These findings have helped scientific understanding of sea level changes along the eastern seaboard and the antiquity of aboriginal presence in the Sydney area.

Next is the Hawthorne Canal. After much discussion in the 1890's, a navigable canal from the Parramatta

River to Marion Street in Sydney was opened. A commuter ferry service began in 1903 with numerous ferries leaving the Haberfield Wharf daily for the city. However, this ferry service was soon abandoned due to the sedimentation of the canal and competition from nearby train services. Today, the canal is a local beauty spot and an area where many people ramble and exercise their dogs.

Finally, I'd like to mention the Sale Canal, which is the longest canal in Australia. About five kilometres long, it was dug in the period 1886 to 1890 to connect the town of Sale with the Gippsland Lakes and thence to the Bass Strait. The Sale Canal is the only canal in Australia that has double canal lanes, which allows for unhindered traffic both ways.

That is the end of section two. You will now have half a minute to check your answers.

(30-second gap)

Now turn to section three.

Section three. You will hear two students discussing their psychology course with a tutor. First you have some time to look at questions twenty-one to twenty-six.

(20-second gap)

Now listen carefully and answer questions twenty-one to twenty-six.

Daniel		Hello, Dr. Peters. Can we have a moment of your time?

Dr. Peters	Hello, Daniel. Hello, Georgia. Yes, I'm free. What can I do for you?

Georgia		It's to do with next year. As you know, we've finished our first year of the Psychology course and we've got some questions about next year's course and what we should do.

Dr. Peters	You're both doing the BSc, is that right?

Daniel		Yes, that's right.

Dr. Peters	Good. That means you will now have a sound foundation for understanding the basic principles of psychological theory and analysis used in social sciences. Did you do plenty of experiments?

Georgia		Yes, we did loads, especially in Behavioural Neuroscience.

Dr. Peters	Well, in your second year, you'll cover material in depth from the remaining key areas of Psychology, which are Cognitive Psychology and Perception, Developmental Psychology and Social Psychology.

Daniel		Will we continue to learn about research methods?

Dr. Peters	Oh yes. You'll need that in preparation for the final year project.

Georgia		Will the third year be similar?

Dr. Peters	In your third and final year, you'll widen your knowledge in Clinical Psychology. We will also offer a wide selection of modules allowing you to specialise in whichever area of Psychology you are particularly interested in. This can include Health Psychology, Clinical Psychology, Educational Psychology, Social Psychology, Developmental Psychopathology, Forensic Psychology, Perception and many more.

Daniel	I heard that students can also choose something outside Psychology.
Dr. Peters	That's right. Psychology is so multi-disciplinary that people often want to combine it with studies of other areas of society. We therefore also permit our students to choose up to two <u>options</u> outside of Psychology, facilitating this interdisciplinary study.
Georgia	And do you think that this helps students with getting a job after their course?
Dr. Peters	Well, although some psychology graduates become professional psychologists, many others go on to work in related fields and the other things that psychology students study can help a lot. Psychology involves the application of a reasoned approach, problem solving and manipulation of data, all of which are <u>scientific aspects</u> that can be useful tools for careers in healthcare, law enforcement, finance, IT and research. Industry research has proved this and also job descriptions for vacant positions also regularly list these qualities as required or preferred skills. Students' knowledge of <u>motivation</u>, their ability to critically analyse a problem, formulate a considered response, create an argument and generate new ideas lend themselves well to careers in the creative industries, the legal sector, government administration and education.
Daniel	So, you think there are lots of things open to us?
Dr. Peters	Oh yes!

You now have some time to look at questions twenty-seven to thirty.

(20-second gap)

Now listen to the rest of the discussion and answer questions twenty-seven to thirty.

Daniel	So, Dr. Peters. Do we have to write a dissertation in year two or year three?
Dr. Peters	We call it a research paper and it's in year three. All BSc Psychology students must also choose a topic and research question for their research paper. When they have decided on their topic and research question, they will need to present their ideas to a member of the Psychology teaching staff, so that someone can agree to be their <u>supervisor</u>. The research paper is the culmination of three years of research training and will constitute a valuable piece of psychological research, the best example of which will have a <u>prize</u> awarded. It's hard work and not much time for holidays!
Georgia	So, how is the study for the research paper done?
Dr. Peters	Teaching in this unit is done via individual meetings. These contact hours are recommended to be around fifteen hours. The main part of the study though will be you on your own and this is recommended to be around a hundred and thirty-five hours.
Daniel	That's a lot.
Dr. Peters	Oh yes. In order to succeed students need to show a considerable degree of <u>self-discipline</u>. A lot of research and reading will need to be done and you'll need to be able to summarise key theoretical and empirical findings and identify how future research can develop and address key questions in the area that you choose.
Georgia	Do many students struggle with the research paper?

Dr. Peters	At some point, most students have varying degrees of difficulty, but that's why it's a key part of the course. By overcoming the problems, students develop significant personal and study skills. Oh, I forgot to add that you need to include a <u>literature review</u>, which is an important part of a research paper.
Daniel	What does that entail?
Dr. Peters	Its aim is to help you to read and write broadly about theory and research related to your Empirical Project. You will have to review and summarise existing research and papers in the subject you have chosen.
Georgia	Well, thanks, Dr. Peters. I think that's enough to be going on with.
Daniel	Yes, thanks, Dr. Peters.
Dr. Peters	You're welcome. See you later.
Georgia	Yes, goodbye.
Daniel	Goodbye.

That is the end of section three. You will now have half a minute to check your answers.

(30-second gap)

Now turn to section four.

Section four. You will hear part of a conservation lecture on aviation pollution in the UK. First you have some time to look at questions thirty-one to forty.

(50-second gap)

Now listen carefully and answer questions thirty-one to forty.

Good evening. In this environmental protection lecture, we are going to discuss the pollution concerns created by the United Kingdom's aviation industry.

Last year, over two hundred million passengers passed through mainland UK airports. This was a return to growth, following a <u>decline</u> in passenger numbers and air transport movements over the previous four years. <u>Forecasts</u> predict that this will rise by twenty-five per cent over the next five years and by fifty per cent over the next ten years.

Airport operations are an important factor in the UK's economy, for tourism, imports, exports and business. However, these benefits must be weighed against the impact air travel is having on the <u>quality of life</u> of increasing numbers of people and on the local and global environments. Noise and air pollution, both from aircraft and from airport ground operations, are a problem for those who live, work and study around airports.

The most immediate impact of aircraft is noise, whether it is the regular rumble of international jets or the buzz of microlights and light aircraft on sunny afternoons. The noise from airborne aircraft is related to <u>speed</u>. Any fast-moving components, such as propellers and compressor blades, generate noise, as do the exhaust gases of jets.

Aircraft are also responsible for an increasing proportion of air pollutant emissions, both at local and global levels. Aircraft engines generally combust fuel efficiently, and jet exhausts have very low smoke emissions. However, pollutant emissions from aircraft are increasing with rising aircraft traffic. In addition, a large amount of air pollution around airports is exacerbated by surface traffic.

ICAO, The International Civil Aviation Organisation, has fixed international standards for smoke and certain gaseous pollutants for newly produced large jet engines and it also restricts the venting of fuel. Reductions in emissions from aircraft engines have also generally been lower in recent years than in other sectors, where technologies such as exhaust gas recirculation have been employed.

Aviation is also a significant source of carbon dioxide emissions, and presents a major threat to UK government targets. This is for three reasons. Firstly, aviation is predicted to grow significantly, and secondly, emissions at altitude are thought to have a greater effect on climate change than those at ground level, and finally, there is no practical alternative to kerosene-fuelled jet engines currently on the horizon. As other sectors reduce emissions, aviation is therefore likely to become responsible for a far larger proportion of global climate change emissions.

The UK government is therefore seeking to reduce the environmental and social harm arising from aviation through a balanced programme of progressive introduction of improved technology, better operational practice and demand management. However, successful action to reduce the environmental and social harm caused by aviation will require cooperation between the UK and other countries. The UK government should adopt a leading and active role in international debate, particularly in partnership with the European Union, and should encourage the development of radical and innovative solutions.

The emission gases from civil aviation that cause the most worries are carbon dioxide, carbon monoxide, nitric oxide and nitrogen dioxide, though there are of course particulate emissions, such as sulfates and, most importantly, black carbon. Aircraft black carbon emissions contribute to the greenhouse effect, but because there is almost no accurate historical data of black carbon emitted by aircraft at cruise, its significance is not fully understood. For the majority of aircraft engines, the only black carbon-related measurement currently available is smoke number, which is a filter based optical method designed to measure near-ground black carbon presence. This, however, does not measure aircraft emissions at cruise level. Passenger jets fly in the stratosphere, which is above the troposphere, the atmosphere layer going from the ground up to around thirty kilometres. The extremely wide mesosphere is above the stratosphere, but no passenger jets go that high. Jets of course spend most of their journeys at their cruise altitudes, and so it's important to develop a method that measures how much black carbon and other emissions are left behind aircraft and what their effects are at that altitude. There is a technique just developed known as first order approximation, which approximates black carbon mass emissions at cruise level, but the rough nature of the measurements makes them unreliable and it has already been proven that the measurements underestimate the emission levels. UK aviation authorities are therefore currently being urged to find out ways of accurately measuring the levels and effects of black carbon emitted at cruise altitudes.

That is the end of section four. You will now have half a minute to check your answers.

(30-second gap)

This is the end of listening test twenty-two. In the IELTS test you would now have ten minutes to transfer your answers to the listening answer sheet.

LISTENING TEST 23 TRANSCRIPT

This recording is copyright.

IELTS-Blog.com listening practice tests. Test twenty-three. In the IELTS test you hear some recordings and you have to answer questions on them. You have time to read the instructions and questions and check your work. All recordings are played only once. The test is in four sections. Now turn to section one.

Section one. You will hear a conversation between a man and a woman discussing the first day at a new job for the woman.

First you have some time to look at questions one to five.

(20-second gap)

Now the full test will begin. You should answer the questions as you listen, as the recording is not played twice. Listen carefully to the conversation and answer questions one to five.

Robert	Hi Louisa. Thanks for coming in.
Louisa	No problem, Robert. What do you need from me?
Robert	Well, as you're starting work here at Group 8 security in a couple of days, I have to get you registered in our security system. First, I need to get some information from you.
Louisa	No problem. What do you need first?
Robert	We'll start with your date of birth.
Louisa	It's the 4th of April 1994.
Robert	And what's your full name?
Louisa	It's Louisa Jennifer Griffiths.
Robert	How do you spell Griffiths?
Louisa	G - R - I, double F, I - T - H - S.
Robert	Thank you. And what's your full address?
Louisa	45 Sherborne Road, Greenham.
Robert	What's the postcode for that address?
Louisa	It's GH6 7HY.
Robert	Can I take a phone number for you?
Louisa	Of course. My home phone number is 01483 759 742.
Robert	Can I have your cell phone number as well, as that's often much easier to use?
Louisa	Of course. My cell number is 07854 375 986.

Robert	Can you say that number again, please?
Louisa	07854 375 986.
Robert	Now, am I right in saying that you're entering the company at <u>grade 5</u>?
Louisa	Yes, that's correct.
Robert	And do you know yet in which section you'll be?
Louisa	To start with, I'm with home security, on <u>the 4th floor</u>.
Robert	Thanks. That's all the basics done.

Before the conversation continues, you have some time to look at questions six to ten.

(20-second gap)

Now listen carefully and answer questions six to ten.

Robert   So, now I'd like to tell you what to do on your first day here.

Louisa   Yes, that would be useful.

Robert   You should try to arrive at around eight in the morning. When you first come in, go to the reception and ask for Anna. She'll be expecting you and will give you your <u>ID badge</u>. This will give you access to all parts of the building.

Louisa   Do I need to give you a photo?

Robert   No. The one on your application form was fine and we've used that. After meeting Anna, go to the fourth floor, where your department head will meet you. He'll give you a quick tour of your department and then the whole building. Then, at ten o'clock, go to the meeting room on the eighth floor, where you'll have a two-hour orientation. You'll do things like giving your <u>social security number</u> and bank details for your salary. You'll receive your passwords for the computers and copiers and there will also be legal papers to sign and various other pieces of paperwork to deal with.

Louisa   At my last job I used to bring in a flask of coffee for myself. Can I do that here?

Robert   Sure, if you want to. We have drinks stations on every floor though, and there is tea, coffee, water and juices freely available all day, so you don't need to bring in anything yourself. There are also <u>rolls</u> there, in case you need a snack during the day.

Louisa   That's very useful.

Robert   We have a canteen in the basement, where there are subsidised meals available. You can go there for lunch after your orientation. Most staff go there for lunch as it's cheap and the food is quite good. Sometimes people eat out for a change, though.

Louisa   Well, I'll definitely try it out at first.

Robert   After lunch, you'll go back to your department and you'll be shown where you'll be working. I expect your department will get you looking at the initial <u>project</u> that you'll be working on.

Louisa	What are the actual hours that I need to be here?
Robert	It really depends on the project that you're working on, but as a general rule, we start here between seven and ten in the morning and people leave between four and seven in the evening. Lunch can be taken any time between eleven and three. As long as you do your contracted eight hours a day, you can start and finish quite flexibly.
Louisa	Do I need to sign in and out every day?
Robert	You swipe your ID every time you enter and leave the building, so signing in and out is all done automatically. This is also helpful, as it allows us to know who's in the building at any one time in case of a fire.

That is the end of section one. You will now have half a minute to check your answers.

(30-second gap)

Now turn to section two.

Section two. You will hear a woman presenting a radio show on mountain gorillas. First you have some time to look at questions eleven to fifteen.

(20-second gap)

Now listen carefully to the radio show and answer questions eleven to fifteen.

Good morning ladies and gentlemen. My name is Linda Wilkinson and I've been invited in today to talk about the endangered mountain gorilla. Few animals capture the imagination more than this extraordinary creature, but tragically its numbers are woefully small. However, what might have been a depressing future for the mountain gorilla just a couple of decades ago has brightened in recent years due to conservation efforts. This isn't to say that the situation isn't still very, very frightening. Right now, the overall mountain gorilla population is approximately eight hundred, an increase from the seven hundred and eighty six estimated two years ago. Gorillas, like all wild animals, play an important role in their environment. Without these large-scale grazers eating lots of vegetation, the natural equilibrium in the food chain would be disrupted.

There are various reasons why the mountain gorillas have become so endangered. To start with, they live in a very challenging environment with extreme cold from the elevation of where they live. Then, although the mountain gorilla was not even known to science until 1902, a combination of hunting, disease and habitat destruction has driven this very rare primate to the verge of extinction. We are happy to say though that despite ongoing civil conflict, continued poaching and an encroaching human population, populations of mountain gorillas have had this increase in numbers.

Many people believe that the habitat reduction has led to a problem in finding prey, but it is perhaps surprising that an animal as large and strong as the mountain gorilla is primarily a herbivore. They eat over a hundred different species of plants and they rarely need to drink, since their diet is so rich in herbs from which they get their water. Other things that they eat include leaves, shoots, and stems of herbaceous vegetation. These plants are all easily found in the types of mountainous forests where the gorilla is found.

Habitat loss is one of the most severe threats to gorilla populations and the forests where mountain gorillas live are surrounded by rapidly increasing human settlements. The main issue leading to habitat loss is that, as humans have moved into areas near mountain gorillas, they have cleared land, so that farming can expand. Even land within protected areas is not safe from clearing, for example, three years ago, illegal settlers cleared three thousand and seven hundred acres of mountain gorilla forest in one prominent National Park. In addition to this, inside mountain gorilla habitats, people utilise charcoal for cooking and heating, and habitat clearance to produce this has also led to the destruction of a lot of the areas where mountain gorilla live.

You now have some time to look at questions sixteen to twenty.

(20-second gap)

Now listen to the rest of the radio show and answer questions sixteen to twenty.

I'd like now to tell you a little bit about the organisation I work with, which is called Life Plus. We work with a variety of endangered animals, including the mountain gorilla. Recently, we've actually been able to buy some mountain gorilla habitat in Rwanda and we're developing a protection and development program that will allow us to nurture the mountain gorilla population living in our area.

I'd like now to tell you something about the gorillas in our care. I find our gorillas just like people and their characters are as clear to me now as the characters of my own friends.

The most imposing character is definitely Simba and he's the dominant male in our group. Simba of course means lion in Swahili and we gave him this name because of his imposing bulk. Because of his size and demeanor, you'd expect Simba to be highly aggressive, but, although he can be with other males who challenge him, he is incredibly compassionate and is often the first of the group to comfort others in distress, for example if they're sick.

The prettiest of our gorillas is Linda. She's three years old and is a very popular sight for tourists who visit our area. She's not that easy to find or see, because she is wary of visitors and will often disappear into the undergrowth if she hears or sees the telltale signs of a group approaching her. Linda has recently become a mother and so she's become an even more popular sight. We of course have to restrict how often people view her, as we don't want to distress her in any way now that she's caring for her baby.

The opposite to Linda is Jojo. She enjoys having tourists close by and, although we always try and keep our distance, Jojo will often try and get close. This is wonderful for our visitors, who get to see a gorilla close up and it gives them great opportunities to get some great snapshots.

Our largest female is Leila, but we're a bit worried about her. The last time she was spotted, it was noted that she was pregnant. Since then, she's gone out of sight for a couple of weeks. She's not that old and she didn't seem as though she was sick, but until we see her again, we'll continue to be a little concerned. It's not that unusual behaviour though, so we're expecting everything to be alright.

A lot of people's favourite is Tommo. He's full of drive and vigor and he's always playing with the others, and climbing and running. He's one that really needs to sleep well at night, so that he can continue his crazy lifestyle during the day!

That is the end of section two. You will now have half a minute to check your answers.

(30-second gap)

Now turn to section three.

Section three. You will hear three students discussing arrangements for a geography field trip. First you have some time to look at questions twenty-one to twenty-five.

(20-second gap)

Now listen carefully and answer questions twenty-one to twenty-five.

Lizzie   Hi Sally. Hi Chris. Are you looking for me?

Sally   Hi Lizzie. Yes, we are. We wanted to go through the arrangements for our geography field trip to Wales. Are you free?

Lizzie   Yes, I am. That's a good idea. Sit down here.

Chris   So, shall I start? The trip will start on the 18th of June, which is a Monday. I suggest we meet in front of the student launderette on Manchester Road. I think we should get an early start and leave at five a.m. That way we can do three hours' driving before the rush hour starts. I reckon that it will then take a further 2 hours to drive to Conway in north Wales, which is where we'll be staying.

Sally   And what will we do when rush hour starts?

Chris   I thought we'd all be ready to pause by then. The drivers certainly will be. I think we should pause at a café and have breakfast or just a drink and then get going again at around nine thirty. Then we'd get to Conway at around midday if we're lucky with the traffic.

Lizzie   That sounds like a good plan. Who's going to drive?

Sally   I'm in charge of transport. As there will be twelve of us all together, I've booked a fourteen-seater minibus. It should be big enough for all of us and all our luggage. Chris and Jennifer have offered to drive.

Lizzie   I can do some driving too, if you want.

Sally   Thanks Lizzie, but the problem is that you have to be twenty-three years old or older to drive the minibus and I know that you're twenty-one like me. That's why I didn't ask you already. Only Chris and Jennifer are old enough.

Lizzie   How much will the transport cost?

Sally   We have the minibus for a week. We only need it for 6 days, but the deal for a week was cheaper than for six days. Six days was four hundred and fifty pounds, but a week was four hundred and eight pounds. Another company I checked was cheaper at three hundred and fifty pounds, but I was warned off them.

Lizzie   So that only comes to thirty-four pounds each. That's a great price!

Sally   I thought so.

Lizzie   And what about the field trip arrangements once we're there?

Chris	I've organised that bit as well. We'll be there four nights, so we come back on Friday afternoon. On Monday afternoon, as we only have a half day, we're going to stay in town and do the research on the beach and town development. There will be three groups of four. I don't have the exact list with me, as I left it at home, but it's all done. We can do the beach measurements, and interview some of the hotel and shop owners. The town museum knows we're coming, and they'll have lots of historical data in their records for us.
Lizzie	And the other days?
Chris	On Tuesday, we're due at Manor Farm for the whole day. They're almost unique, as the farm's topography goes from quite high hills right down to the sea's edge.
Lizzie	And Wednesday?
Chris	We drive inland from the sea and we'll meet a guide to take us up into the north Wales mountains, where we'll spend the day. We'll focus on a valley about an hour's walk from the road. The valley has a small river running through it and its other features will be perfect for the type of research that we need to do.
Sally	What will we do for food that day? I suppose there won't be any shops nearby.
Chris	We'll have breakfast at the hostel and then they'll give us a packed lunch for the day. We'll be back at the hostel in time for dinner.
Sally	And what will we do on Thursday?
Chris	We'll look at the historical section of our trip. Part of what we need to do is to analyse the geographical implications of historical settlements. Conway has an old castle and so we can spend the day in and around it and do our research. The castle also has a museum and that will help us with some aspects of this study.
Lizzie	What about Friday morning, as we don't leave until lunchtime?
Chris	We'll have the morning free. Probably, we'll just need that time to collate and organise all our work that we'll have done over the week.

You now have some time to look at questions twenty-six to thirty.

(20-second gap)

Now listen to the rest of the discussion and answer questions twenty-six to thirty.

Sally	So, Lizzie. You were in charge of accommodation at the hostel. What have you sorted out?
Lizzie	The hostel does not have small rooms, so we'll have to be together in small dormitories. The girls are on the first floor. Sally, you, Jennifer and I will be in room three, which is first on the right after you come up the stairs from the ground floor. It has three single beds. It's quite small, but it does have an ensuite bathroom, with a separate bath and shower and also a toilet. The second girls' room is room two, which is on the left after you come up the stairs. It's for Sarah, Angela, and Wendy. There is one single bed and one bunk bed there.
Chris	We boys will be on the second floor, then.
Lizzie	That's right. You have the same two rooms as the girls, but one floor up. The smaller room with the ensuite is for you, Simon and Sebastian, and the larger room is for Robin, Alex and Leon. They have a

bigger room, but they'll need to use the communal bathroom, which is on the left when you come out of their room. That's the same for the girls below. You boys will have the advantage of full computer use, but apparently the router can't operate correctly on the girls' floor, so we'll have to do without. The dining room is on the third floor, so everyone will need to go there in order to get breakfast.

Chris   When are the meals?

Lizzie   Breakfast is from half past six until half past eight. They don't do lunch apart from packed lunches. Dinner is from six until eight. There's a bell to indicate the start of both meals. It will be fairly plain food, but they told me there'll be plenty of it!

Sally   Is there any security at the hostel?

Lizzie   Yes. We will get keys for all the rooms, though we need to give the hostel a deposit for each key. At night, the front doors are locked from eleven p.m. They are unlocked from six a.m. When the doors are unlocked, there's always someone on duty in the reception.

Chris   Anything else?

Lizzie   If we've got any energy left at the end of the day, the hostel organises walks around the town in the evening. We can join that or watch a film. They show a film every evening in the common room.

Sally   Well, it seems as though most things are organised. Shall we go off to our next class now?

That is the end of section three. You will now have half a minute to check your answers.

(30-second gap)

Now turn to section four.

Section four. You will hear part of a lecture on alternative power sources. First you have some time to look at questions thirty-one to forty.

(50-second gap)

Now listen carefully and answer questions thirty-one to forty.

Good morning and welcome to this lecture on alternative power sources. As you know, we've been focusing recently on solar power and today we want to continue this theme by looking at how solar energy can be harnessed to power planes.

Solar aviation began with model aircrafts in the 1970's, when affordable solar cells appeared on the market. However, it was not until 1980 that the first human flights were realised. The Solar Challenger, with a maximum power of two point five kilowatts, succeeded in crossing the English Channel on its maiden flight in suspect weather in 1981 and continued across France covering distances of several hundred kilometers, landing only for service checks. By the end, the battery was exhausted, but its mission had been completed. In 1990, the American-built Sunseeker crossed the United States in twenty-one stages and one hundred and twenty-one flying hours over a period of almost two months.

In the middle of the 1990's, several airplanes were built to participate in the 'Berblinger' competition. Since 1988, the town of Ulm has been awarding the Berblinger Prize from time to time as a tribute to the work of Albrecht Ludwig Berblinger, the 'Tailor of Ulm', and his attempt to fly across the Danube in 1811. This prize is awarded for original inventive and creative ideas in the field of general aviation, with a focus of interest on safety, environmental sustainability, aerodynamics, construction design and economy. The aim was to be able to climb to an altitude of four hundred and fifty metres with the aid of batteries and to maintain horizontal flight with solar energy power of at least five hundred watts per square metre, which corresponds to about half of the power emitted by the sun at midday on the equator.

One must not also forget Helios, developed by another American company for NASA. This remote-controlled unmanned aircraft, with a wingspan of more than seventy metres, established a record altitude of nearly thirty thousand meters in 2001. Surprise turbulence during a later flight led to its break up, and it crashed into the Pacific Ocean.

Recently, a Swiss team developed the Solar Impulse, a solar powered design that has taken the ideas of the early pioneers and developed solar powered planes to an unprecedented level. The Solar Impulse HBSIA prototype presents physical and aerodynamic features never seen before, with its huge wingspan equal to that of an Airbus A340, yet only as heavy as an average car. These factors place the Solar Impulse in a yet unexplored flight envelope.

With two hundred square metres of photovoltaic cells and a twelve per cent total efficiency of the propulsion chain, the plane's motors achieve an average power of eight horsepower or six kilowatts. That's roughly the amount of power the Wright brothers had available to them in 1903 when they made their first powered flight. And it is with that energy, optimised from the solar panel to the propeller, that Solar Impulse has managed to fly day and night without fuel!

The twelve thousand or so photovoltaic cells of one hundred and forty-five microns of monocrystalline silicon combine lightness and efficiency. Their efficiency could have been even higher, like the panels used in space, but their weight would then have been much too high, penalising the plane during the night flight. This phase is the most critical and the plane's batteries must be fully charged. The batteries are the main constraint in the plane's design and they require a drastic reduction of the weight of the rest of the plane, so as to optimise the whole energy chain and to maximise the aerodynamic performance provided by using a high aspect ratio wing alongside a low speed profile.

Four pods are fixed under the wings. Each contains a brushless, sensorless electric motor, a polymer lithium battery consisting of seventy accumulators, and a management system controlling the change in temperature thresholds. The insulation has been designed to conserve the heat radiated by the batteries and keep them functioning despite the minus forty degrees Celsius encountered at eight thousand five hundred meters. Each motor has a maximum power output of ten horsepower.

The solar impulse's batteries work like most other solar batteries. Pointed towards the sun, solar panels capture the energy in sunlight and convert it directly to DC electricity, which is passed down to the charge controller, which operates the solar array at its maximum efficiency and feeds the electricity into the battery bank. It also protects the battery bank from overcharging, as when the battery bank is fully charged, it interrupts the flow of electricity from the solar panels. Batteries are expensive and lose potency when under or over-charged, so this process extends the life of the batteries. Finally, as DC current is usually not needed, the inverter transforms the solar-produced DC electricity into the AC electricity commonly used.

That is the end of section four. You will now have half a minute to check your answers.

(30-second gap)

This is the end of listening test twenty-three. In the IELTS test you would now have ten minutes to transfer your answers to the listening answer sheet.

LISTENING TEST 24 TRANSCRIPT

This recording is copyright.

IELTS-Blog.com listening practice tests. Test twenty-four. In the IELTS test you hear some recordings and you have to answer questions on them. You have time to read the instructions and questions and check your work. All recordings are played only once. The test is in four sections. Now turn to section one.

Section one. You will hear a conversation between a man and a woman as the woman organises a change in her family's dentist.

First you have some time to look at questions one to five.

(20-second gap)

Now the full test will begin. You should answer the questions as you listen, as the recording is not played twice. Listen carefully to the conversation and answer questions one to five.

Robert   Good morning, Madam, and welcome to Albans Dental Practice. My name's Robert. What can I do for you today?

Margaret   Hello, Robert. I'm Margaret. My family and I have just moved to the area and I need to register with a new dentist for all of us.

Robert   That's fine. We have space on our books. What's the name of your family?

Margaret   It's Wood. That's W – O – O – D. As I said, I'm Margaret and my husband's name is Gareth.

Robert   Thank you. Is he here today?

Margaret   No. He had to go into work today.

Robert   Not to worry. Now, do you have dental insurance for your family?

Margaret   No, but we heard that we can sign up for insurance with you and that's what we'd like to do.

Robert   That's fine. So, I'll need some information about your family first. Who is there and how old are they?

Margaret   Well, first of all, there's me and my husband and I've given you our first names already. He's forty-two and I'm forty.

Robert   And what about the details of your children?

Margaret   We have a son and a daughter. My son's called Tim, and he's ten years old. My daughter is Amelia, and she's <u>twelve</u>.

Robert   Will we be able to access your family's dental records from your previous dentist?

Margaret   Oh yes. We spoke to our previous practice about that and they said that when we'd found a new practice, we should give them your <u>email</u> address and they'd send you everything.

Robert	Good. That'll be very helpful. What was the name of the previous dentist?
Margaret	It was Mr. Harding and his practice was in north London.
Robert	I don't know that practice off the top of my head, but that's not important. Have you found a permanent address yet?
Margaret	Not yet, but we put an <u>offer</u> in on a place and we're confident it'll be accepted.
Robert	That'll be a relief I expect. Where's the house?
Margaret	It's in Winton Woods.
Robert	Ah yes. That's not far at all from here, is it?
Margaret	No, it's just around the corner and that's one of the reasons why we chose this practice.
Robert	So, what's the best way to contact you?
Margaret	Our mobile phones probably. My number's 07763 849 662 and my husband's number is 07763 854 <u>118</u>.
Robert	Can you say your husband's number again?
Margaret	It's 07763 854 double 1 8.
Robert	Thanks very much.

Before the conversation continues, you have some time to look at questions six to ten

(20-second gap)

Now listen carefully and answer questions six to ten.

Margaret	Now, can you let me know a little bit about the dental insurance that you offer?
Robert	We have two plans on offer, a core plan and a premium plan. The core plan includes <u>routine check-ups</u>, hygiene treatments, gum disease treatments and dental x-rays.
Margaret	What about remedial treatment?
Robert	That's partially covered by the core plan. You get fifty per cent of all costs paid on remedial or restorative treatments such as fillings, crowns, bridges and dentures. I can give you a paper with an exhaustive list of what you can get with the core plan.
Margaret	Thank you.
Robert	Finally, there is a mouth cancer cover, with up to twelve thousand pounds towards charges for one course of treatment per person for up to eighteen months after <u>diagnosis</u>. Smokers are included in this.
Margaret	Well, none of us is a smoker, but that would be good to have just in case.
Robert	What's also very handy is that the insurance covers you when you travel overseas. There is worldwide dental accident cover with up to five thousand pounds cover for dental accident treatment for

up to four incidents.

Margaret That's useful as we travel a few times a year as a family. What about cleaning?

Robert No, that's not covered.

Margaret How is the premium plan better?

Robert You obviously get all the benefits of the core plan, but the big difference is that all costs are covered for remedial treatment. The overseas treatment cover is also increased to <u>ten thousand</u> pounds.

Margaret Is cleaning covered with the premium cover?

Robert Yes, it is, and another important part of the premium plan is that tooth straightening procedures for children are available on it, so if your children need braces, that's covered.

Margaret Is it important for children to have braces?

Robert Sometimes. It can allow children to <u>bite</u> correctly, eat more comfortably, and care for their teeth and gums more easily.

Margaret Do they have to wear the braces for a long time?

Robert Braces treatment usually lasts from eighteen months to two years, and visits to the dentist are needed every four to six weeks.

Margaret What are the costs of the plans?

Robert All our plans are fixed on <u>monthly payments</u>. The core plan is thirty pounds per person and the premium plan is forty-five pounds per person. As you're a family, a family policy can be obtained for a hundred pounds a month for the core plan and a hundred and fifty pounds for the premium plan.

Margaret Well, my husband's company will pay, but I'm not sure which policy they'll cover. I'll have to ask.

Robert That's fine. Drop in when you find out and decide.

That is the end of section one. You will now have half a minute to check your answers.

(30-second gap)

Now turn to section two.

Section two. You will hear a woman giving an introductory talk about an exercise club. First you have some time to look at questions eleven to fifteen.

(20-second gap)

Now listen carefully to the introductory talk and answer questions eleven to fifteen.

Hello and welcome everyone to this information talk on the Yardley Exercise Club. We're a group of people who want to get fit and we also want to have fun and be sociable whilst doing it.

Our exercise structure is that we have a different exercise type done every day from Monday to Thursday. We don't usually have anything planned at weekends, but we do from time to time. Members of the club can just turn up and join in. There is a nominated planner for each day, so that no one person has to do too much organisational work.

As I said earlier, this is a sociable club. Every month, one of our members opens her or his house to everyone and we meet up for a barbecue, pizza evening, curry night or whatever the host has chosen. People pay a modest fee for these evenings to the host to cover food and drinks.

The membership charge is ten pounds a month and it ought to be paid by bank transfer on the first day of every month. This money is used for any bookings to be done and for insurance. No-one in the club actually takes any money out of the club. Once you've joined, you need to make sure that your email address and mobile phone number are sent to Jack Lane, as he makes sure that your details are added to the email and mobile lists. Everyone gets a mail and a text message on Sunday every week. The mail explains what the plan for the week is, although the plan is on our website as well of course.

Before I start talking about our exercise activities, make a note that all the exercise activities start at seven p.m. from Monday to Thursday. Please arrive early to avoid injury. Every activity starts with some warming-up exercises. In case people do get injured, one of the members present will be trained and will have our first aid kit with him or her.

You now have some time to look at questions sixteen to twenty.

(20-second gap)

Now listen to the rest of the introductory talk and answer questions sixteen to twenty.

On Mondays, we go running. Albert is the organiser for this and he chooses a run each week that can be five or eight kilometres long. We have some routes we always use, so you'll get to know where to go once you've done the runs a few times.

Tuesday is our swimming day. Alison has a regular booking at the Yardley Sports Club for two lanes for an hour in their pool. One lane is designated as slow and the other is for medium or fast. Swimmers are recommended to bring goggles if they want to join this activity, as the necessary levels of chlorine in the pool can irritate some people's eyes.

On Wednesdays, we go cycling. Stan is the organiser and he plans reasonably challenging routes for us away from traffic. If you don't have a bike, you can hire one at a discount from Yardley Bikes. Just say you're a member. In the winter, the cycling activity takes place at the Yardley Cycling Track, as the roads can be very dark and this could result in an accident.

On Thursdays, Jo has a fixed booking at the Yardley Sports Centre again, but this time in the gym. We have an hour's weight and circuit training there. This is probably the toughest challenge of the week, but if you take it easy and build yourself up, you'll be surprised how quickly you get stronger and faster.

That is the end of section two. You will now have half a minute to check your answers.

(30-second gap)

Now turn to section three.

Section three. You will hear a university professor dealing with a student complaint. First you have some time to look at questions twenty-one to twenty-five.

(20-second gap)

Now listen carefully and answer questions twenty-one to twenty-five.

Prof. Williams   Good morning, Jonathan. What can I do for you today?

Jonathan   Good morning, Professor Williams. Well, it's a bit embarrassing really, but I'd like to complain about something.

Prof. Williams   Really! Well, you'd better tell me about it then. Is there a problem about me?

Jonathan   No, it's about the unit I'm doing with Dr. Forrest. Now, Dr. Forrest gives my favourite course and he's a pretty good teacher. However, it's regarding my last essay. You see, he told us that he would not accept any emailed submissions for his latest essay on hydrothermal vents. He wanted us all to place a printed copy in his pigeon hole. Now, we all did this, but he's told us that I and two other students did not give their essays in on time and he's given us a zero. We will all lose our good grade average with this.

Prof. Williams   Do you have any evidence that you three gave in your essays?

Jonathan   No, we don't, but then of course it's hard to show evidence for that. As you know, the university policy nowadays is that students should hand in work digitally, so we were really helping him out.

Prof. Williams   I see. Do you have the three essays with you today?

Jonathan   Yes, I do. They're here.

Prof. Williams   I'll have a word with Dr. Forrest. He's usually pretty reasonable, so I expect they'll be no problem. Anything else?

Jonathan   I'm afraid so. Dr. Forrest is often late, he often finishes too early and from time to time he gets carried away and swears. It gets a bit embarrassing sometimes.

Prof. Williams   Really!

Jonathan   Yes. And Dr. Forrest is supposed to upload all class work and supporting documentation to the department website, but he never does. As you know, many students like to read the papers on their computers, but, because of this, they don't have that option with Dr. Forrest. If they're sick too, they can't get hold of the right papers. When we remind him about it, he can be quite short-tempered.

Prof. Williams   I'll speak to him about that as well, Jonathan. Thanks for telling me.

You now have some time to look at questions twenty-six to thirty.

(20-second gap)

Now listen to the rest of the discussion and answer questions twenty-six to thirty.

Prof. Williams	So, is everything fine with my course?
Jonathan	I think so. We were all a bit confused about the last lecture, though.
Prof. Williams	That was the one on algal blooms, wasn't it?
Jonathan	Yes. We were unsure about how algal blooms are created.

Prof. Williams   As you know, algae are small plant life within water and algal bloom is a rapid increase in the population of algae in an aquatic system. <u>Nutrients</u> encourage the growth of algae and the main ones contributing to this growth are phosphorus and nitrogen. Runoff and erosion from fertilised agricultural areas, erosion from river banks, river beds, land clearing, and <u>sewage</u> from overflowing systems are the major sources of phosphorus and nitrogen entering waterways. Phosphates then attach themselves to sediments. When water is low in dissolved oxygen, the sediments release the phosphates into the water. This provides the food that encourages the growth of algae. Blooms of algae can also occur when the <u>concentrations</u> of nutrients are fairly low, but blooms are more frequent when these are high.

Jonathan   Isn't temperature important as well?

Prof. Williams   Yes. Algal blooms usually develop during the warmer months of the year or when the water temperature is higher and there is increased light. Temperatures of twenty-five degrees Celsius are optimal for the growth of algae. As a result of this, low sea temperatures prevent algal blooms from persisting through the winter months in <u>temperate regions</u>. Higher water temperatures in tropical regions, however, may cause algal blooms to persist throughout the year.

Jonathan   And can the algal blooms be harmful?

Prof. Williams   Algae can pose a risk to human health because of the toxins they produce. These toxins can damage the liver and neurological system of both humans and animals and in severe cases can cause death. The cell walls of all algae contain contact irritants which can cause gastrointestinal, skin, eye and respiratory irritations to humans and animals.

Jonathan   Thanks very much for that. I'll explain that to my friends and we can ask some more questions in our next seminar if necessary.

Prof. Williams   That'll be fine. Bye then.

Jonathan   Bye.

That is the end of section three. You will now have half a minute to check your answers.

(30-second gap)

Now turn to section four.

Section four. You will hear part of an energy lecture on offshore wind energy. First you have some time to look at questions thirty-one to forty.

(50-second gap)

Now listen carefully and answer questions thirty-one to forty.

In today's lecture on energy, we are going to look a little at certain aspects of the offshore wind energy industry.

The first offshore wind project was installed off the coast of Denmark in 1991. Since that time, commercial-scale offshore wind facilities have been increasing in numbers, mainly in European shallow waters. With the U.S. Department of the Interior's 'Smart from the Start' initiative, wind power projects have now been built offshore the United States. Newer turbine and foundation technology is being developed, so that wind power projects can be built in deeper waters further offshore.

Wind energy has been utilised by humans for more than two thousand years. For example, windmills were often used by farmers and ranchers for pumping water or grinding grain. In modern times, wind energy is mainly used to generate electricity, primarily through the use of wind turbines. All wind turbines operate in the same basic manner. As the wind blows, it flows over the airfoil-shaped blades of wind turbines, causing the turbine blades to spin. The blades are connected to a drive shaft that turns an electric generator to produce electricity. The newest wind turbines are highly technologically advanced, and include a number of engineering and mechanical innovations to help maximise efficiency and increase the production of electricity.

Offshore wind turbines are being used by a number of countries to harness the energy of the strong, consistent winds that are found on the oceans near the United States. In the United States, fifty-three per cent of the nation's population lives in coastal areas, where energy costs and demands are high and land-based renewable energy resources are often limited. Abundant offshore wind resources have the potential to supply immense quantities of renewable energy to major U.S. coastal cities, such as New York City and Boston.

Although the wind speeds in the U.S. are not that high on average, the potential energy produced from wind is directly proportional to the cube of the wind speed. As a result, increased wind speeds of only a few miles per hour can produce a significantly large amount of electricity. For instance, a turbine at a site with an average wind speed of sixteen miles per hour would produce fifty per cent more electricity than at a site with the same turbine and average wind speeds of fourteen miles per hour. This is one reason that developers are interested in pursuing offshore wind energy resources.

Commercial-scale offshore wind facilities are similar to onshore wind facilities and so not much new technology needs to be developed. The wind turbine generators used in offshore environments include modifications, so that their foundation can withstand the harsh environment of the ocean, including storm waves, hurricane-force winds, and even ice flows. Fortunately, anti-corrosion technology to protect the turbines from seawater is already very advanced and effective. Although roughly ninety per cent of the United States' wind energy resource occurs in waters that are too deep for the current turbine technology, engineers are working on new technologies, such as innovative foundations and floating wind turbines, that will transition wind power development into the harsher conditions associated with deeper waters.

Wind turbines, like windmills, are mounted on a tower to capture the most energy. At thirty metres or more above ground, they can take advantage of the faster and less turbulent wind. The engineering and design of offshore wind facilities depends on site-specific conditions, particularly water depth, the geology of the seabed, and wave loading. A steel support is driven into the seabed, supporting the tower and the nacelle, which is a shell that encloses the electronic components. Once the turbine is operational, a yaw drive system turns the nacelle to face into the wind, thereby maximising the amount of electricity produced. A wind sensor connected to the top of the tower moves the nacelle, so that it moves with the changes in wind direction.

Wind turbine blades act much like airplane wings. When the wind blows, a pocket of low-pressure air forms on the downwind side of the blades. The low-pressure air pocket then pulls the blade towards it, causing the rotor to turn. This force is actually much stronger than the wind's force against the front side of the blade. The force causes the rotor to spin like a propeller, and the turning shaft inside the nacelle spins a generator to make electricity. There is also a gearbox before the generator to regulate the rotation.

That is the end of section four. You will now have half a minute to check your answers.

(30-second gap)

This is the end of listening test twenty-four. In the IELTS test you would now have ten minutes to transfer your answers to the listening answer sheet.

LISTENING TEST 25 TRANSCRIPT

This recording is copyright.

IELTS-Blog.com listening practice tests. Test twenty-five. In the IELTS test you hear some recordings and you have to answer questions on them. You have time to read the instructions and questions and check your work. All recordings are played only once. The test is in four sections. Now turn to section one.

Section one. You will hear a conversation between a man and a woman discussing Internet problems and an updated contract.

First you have some time to look at questions one to five.

(20-second gap)

Now the full test will begin. You should answer the questions as you listen, as the recording is not played twice. Listen carefully to the conversation and answer questions one to five.

Tony	Good morning. My name is Tony. Welcome to Netwave.
Sheila	Thank you.
Tony	What can I do for you today?
Sheila	I have an account with you and my Internet is having problems.
Tony	I'm sorry about that. Can I take your name, please?
Sheila	It's Sheila Wilde. That's Wilde spelled with an E at the end.
Tony	Thank you. Do you know your account number?
Sheila	Yes. It's W74962Y.
Tony	Let's get that up on the system. Here we are. Can I just confirm some details with you?
Sheila	Of course.
Tony	Can you let me know your date of birth?
Sheila	It's the 16th March 1975.
Tony	And can you let me know your postcode, please?
Sheila	It's WH5 7JH.
Tony	Thank you. That has confirmed your identity and account. Now, what's wrong with your Internet?
Sheila	It happened at the end of last week. On Wednesday, the connection got slower and slower and then from Friday, we just had no connection at all.
Tony	I'm very sorry about that. It must be very frustrating. Did this go on the whole weekend?

Sheila	Yes, it did.
Tony	We've recently had some problems with <u>wiring</u> and I would imagine it's something to do with that. So, let's see when we can come and get it fixed. How about tomorrow in the afternoon? It's the twelfth of August tomorrow. Is three p.m. OK?
Sheila	Tomorrow's fine, but can we make it an hour later, as I'll be picking up the kids from school?
Tony	Absolutely. <u>Four</u> p.m. it is.

Before the conversation continues, you have some time to look at questions six to ten.

(20-second gap)

Now listen carefully and answer questions six to ten.

Tony	Now, I'm looking at your account and there are some things that have changed since you signed on. We can offer you a better service now. To start with, I can double your <u>bandwidth</u>.
Sheila	That would be great.
Tony	You also have your cable TV and phone usage with our company, but they're not combined. At present, you pay thirty dollars monthly for the Internet, ten dollars for the phone line rental and fifty dollars for the full cable TV package. I can combine those to our Homebase Package, which would come to <u>seventy</u> dollars a month.
Sheila	Well, that makes sense. Are there any drawbacks?
Tony	The only thing we would ask you to do is to extend your contract to <u>two years</u> from today's date. Would that be alright?
Sheila	I'll just have to check with my husband tonight. Can I sign up tomorrow when the Internet gets fixed?
Tony	Oh yes. I'll make sure the <u>engineer</u> has the right paperwork with him. I also see that you pay your bills with us monthly. We can set up a direct debit for you if you'd like.
Sheila	Yes, please. My husband and I were just talking about that. Can I do that now?
Tony	Yes. I just need your bank name, account name and number, and your sort code.
Sheila	I can give that to you now. The bank is Pembroke Chase. The account name is Charles and Sheila Wilde. The number is 73685427. The sort code is 86 63 59.
Tony	I've got all that. Your reference number for this is <u>X49</u>. Is there anything else?
Sheila	No. That's all. Thank you very much.
Tony	You're welcome.

That is the end of section one. You will now have half a minute to check your answers.

(30-second gap)

Now turn to section two.

Section two. You will hear a woman giving an introductory talk about the Burley Bird Watching and Nature Club. First you have some time to look at questions eleven to fifteen.

(20-second gap)

Now listen carefully to the introductory talk and answer questions eleven to fifteen.

Good evening everyone and welcome to this get together evening for the Burley Bird Watching and Nature Club. I hope you all have your information sheets, which will summarise some of the things I will talk about soon. I will begin the evening by giving some basic details about the club for newcomers and then after that, I will give some information about our trip next week to the Edgehill Woods area.

We are a group of enthusiasts who love observing the natural world around us. The club was founded in <u>1962</u> and has always enjoyed a strong membership. We meet where we are today, in the Burley Community Hall, at least once a week on Wednesdays. Meetings begin at 7.30 p.m. and usually last for three hours. Different things happen at our meetings. Sometimes we just sit together and have some tea and catch up with old friends and sometimes we have guest speakers who talk on areas of interest to us. For example, next Wednesday, we have John Walker, who will tell us about the birds and animals he saw during a two-month voyage he made out to the Antarctic continent. I'll tell you more about that later.

It does not cost too much to join our club. There is an annual fee of eighty dollars, although there is a <u>joining fee</u> of sixty dollars for new members. The money can be paid by bank transfer or you can just bring the money in cash to one of our meetings and give it to the club treasurer. The money is spent on administration costs, <u>insurance</u>, rental costs for our meetings and subsidising guest speakers. We go on quite a few trips as well to different places, but these trips incur a further cost. All extra payments related to these trips are to cover our costs. No extra profit is made from them.

Naturally, we have our own website. The site is updated regularly with all the details of our trips and events. There is also a Help Desk, where you can email the club and ask any questions. Our <u>committee</u> consists of seven people and we take turns to answer enquiries. One of the most popular sections of the website is our discussion forum. Members can start a discussion and then other members can comment and add their opinions. You must be a member to contribute to this area of the website. Once you've joined, you'll be given your <u>password</u>, so that you can log in, read and contribute.

You now have some time to look at questions sixteen to twenty.

(20-second gap)

Now listen to the rest of the introductory talk and answer questions sixteen to twenty.

As you know, the club is run by its members, so let me tell you a little about who is responsible for what.

First of all, there's Sally Warner, who's the club president. Sally presides at all club meetings and oversees the schedule of events. <u>She's also the one who writes the monthly newsletter that goes out each month detailing what we've been doing and what we're going to do.</u> Sally is retired from her work now and she's always willing to meet up with new and established members to share her knowledge of where to go and what to see.

Next, we have Steven Roth, who's the club treasurer. Steven receives all club money, including dues, gifts, and receipts from fundraising projects, and he maintains the club's bank account. He also of course pays all the bills after approval from the president and other relevant members. Steven is taking a year's sabbatical from work starting next week, so that he can visit his daughter and new granddaughter in Australia. He's promised to be back and part of the club on his return, though.

One of our key members is Angela Carter, who's the events organiser. She sets up all our trips, locally and further afield. Without her, our club wouldn't be the same. It's not all about hiring minibuses and booking hotels. She has overall management of all aspects of events, including all the health and safety, licensing when relevant and making sure we're protected and covered in the event of an accident.

Finally, Darren Williamson is the club secretary. Darren keeps a permanent record of minutes of all club meetings and a complete, up-to-date membership list, with everyone's address, emails and phone numbers. We ask when you join to give him permission to share these details with other members, so that we can liaise easily in regards to trips and meetings.

I'd now like to tell you about our upcoming trip to the Edgehill Woods area, which has a number of hides, from where we can see some interesting and rare species. So, from the car park, we will move to the first hide, which will be due north through the Edgehill Woods. The first hide is ideally situated, as we can see meadow birds and life, as well as being right next to woodland, which can provide us with a variety of different species. The Edgehill Forest is famous for its deer, so we have a good chance of seeing some grazing early in the morning.

After an hour at the first hide, we'll move east across the Upton Meadow to the next hide. This again is advantageous, as it provides a variety of habitat. We're next to a wood again on one side and on the other we have the bank of the Fingleton Pond and its adjacent marshland. There are also the Fingleton Rocks in the medium distance, which are famous for their nesting hawks. We'll get a closer look at them after an hour, when we go further north to a hide overlooking them. Finally, we cross right back across the meadow and go to our final hide, which is closest to the car park.

That is the end of section two. You will now have half a minute to check your answers.

(30-second gap)

Now turn to section three.

Section three. You will hear a university meeting where the future use of an empty room is decided. First you have some time to look at questions twenty-one to twenty-six.

(20-second gap)

Now listen carefully and answer questions twenty-one to twenty-six.

Dr. Cameron	Good afternoon, everyone. As you know, I'm Dr. Cameron. Today, we four are here to discuss what to do with the new space made on the ground floor by the decommissioning of the lower science laboratory. Let me introduce you to each other. First, on my right we have Mrs. Jones, who is the site manager.
Mrs. Jones	Good afternoon.
Dr. Cameron	On my left, we first have Mrs. Strauss, who is the head of the Science department.

Mrs. Strauss	Good afternoon.
Dr. Cameron	Finally, we have Mike Evans, who is the representative from the student council.
Mike	Hello, everyone.
Dr. Cameron	So, let's start with Mrs. Jones.

Mrs. Jones   Well, my plan is that we use this space to open a new café for the students and staff. The room has large double doors that open out to a grass area and some concrete. In the warmer months, we could have some tables and chairs and some large parasols. Because the science lab has lots of gas appliances there, it shouldn't cost too much to convert part of the room to a small kitchen for food preparation.

Mrs. Strauss   That seems to be quite a practical plan. There are certainly lots of people on the site who need food and drink throughout the day.

Dr. Cameron   What do you think about this proposal, Mike?

Mike   I had another idea. Whilst I agree that there are a lot of people on site that need to be served food, I believe quite a few people, especially students, bring packed lunches onto the campus. This is of course much cheaper and attractive for students. The problem is that, at present, there's no location where people can eat their packed lunches. It's not so bad in summer, when most people just sit on the grass, but in the colder months or wet days, there's nowhere to go. Therefore, I'd like to use the room to be a lounge where people can eat.

Dr. Cameron   That's an interesting proposal. How much would it cost to change the room, do you think?

Mike   I don't know exactly, but it shouldn't be too much. We'd have to organise the decommissioning of all the chemistry-related pipes going into the room to make them safe, but that would be the only large expense. We wouldn't need to make a kitchen or anything, we'd just need plenty of tables and chairs. Having some outside in summer is a great idea, as Mrs. Jones suggested.

Mrs. Jones   It's a nice idea, Mike, but there is one main problem. Students are notoriously messy and if there's a room where they can come and eat their own food, the place will soon become very messy indeed. And this will happen every day. The room will have to be cleaned quite thoroughly every day and with the undoubted mess, it'll probably need tidying up throughout the day as well. Who's going to do all this?

Mike   I thought the regular cleaners could do it.

Mrs. Strauss   It's not as easy as that, Mike. The regular cleaners only come in during the evenings and they have a pretty tight schedule. I doubt there'd be time for them to clean a really messy room properly.

Mrs. Jones   And we only have some caretakers on duty during the day and they're far too busy to clean up after students. I don't think they'd appreciate the idea either!

Mike   Could we take on somebody to do it?

Dr. Cameron   Who's going to pay for that though, Mike? We have some budget allocated to change the room, but we certainly don't have any ongoing money devoted to paying a new member of the cleaning staff.

Mrs. Jones   This is where my plan works better. A café would be financially <u>self-sufficient</u>. The café would have to take on extra staff, but it could pay them out of the revenue that it makes.

You now have some time to look at questions twenty-seven to thirty.

(20-second gap)

Now listen to the rest of the discussion and answer questions twenty-seven to thirty.

Dr. Cameron   Are there any other suggestions for the room?

Mrs. Strauss   I did have one suggestion. As it's been a science room for such a long time, I was hoping that we might be able to retain its use for the science department. As you can imagine, the science department uses many dangerous <u>chemicals</u> and at present we store these things in the individual labs. This is not very efficient and also has some security issues.

Dr. Cameron   What security is used at the moment in the labs?

Mrs. Strauss   Right now, the labs only have <u>dead locks</u> as a safeguard and this isn't really enough security for storing some of the things we have.

Dr. Cameron   Yes, I can see why you're worried about this. It's an important concern.

Mrs. Strauss   Yes, it is. It would cost quite a lot to upgrade the security on all the labs, but if we could make the room in question our storeroom, we would only have to install the extra security in one room.

Mrs. Jones   Would it be harder to make it secure, as the room's on the ground floor?

Mrs. Strauss   In theory, yes, but not in reality. You see the ground floor rooms already have <u>shutters</u> that can be put down with controls in the room. The room can just have these down the whole time. That in conjunction with the extra locks we could install on the windows would be more than enough.

Dr. Cameron   Well, that seems to be a sensible suggestion as well. I'm very happy to see that you've all thought so hard about this and come up with three options that are all very worthy and mostly feasible. The problem is that I see that you're all very keen on your own ideas being adopted, so that gives you all one vote without counting me. That means I get the deciding vote. With such great ideas, I don't want to make a decision too quickly, so I think the best thing is that I think about it until next Monday. To help me, would you please email me your <u>proposals</u>? It doesn't have to be in great detail and if you could get that to me by Thursday afternoon, then I can sit down with the Dean of the College and we can talk through the suggestions together on Friday morning. I will email you with the decision on Monday morning.

That is the end of section three. You will now have half a minute to check your answers.

(30-second gap)

Now turn to section four.

Section four. You will hear part of a materials lecture on old rubber tyres. First you have some time to look at questions thirty-one to forty.

(50-second gap)

Now listen carefully and answer questions thirty-one to forty.

Good morning everyone and welcome to this materials science lecture. We are continuing our unit on recycling and today our focus will be on tyres.

According to the World Business Council for Sustainable Development, a total of one billion end of life tyres are generated every year globally. There are also approximately four billion end of life tyres in landfill and stockpiles globally and, as they do not decompose, they can be a fire risk, which, if not dealt with, can contaminate the air with toxic fumes.

It's hard to dispose of end of life tyres, as chemically cross-linked polymers, either natural or synthetic, are found in them and they do not degrade under natural environmental conditions. One of the hazards of storing them is that these polymers diffuse hazardous chemicals into the surroundings, which can kill many beneficial micro-organisms. This is a significant threat to our ecology and the chemicals are also passed into our food chains.

Stockpiled tyres are also ideal mosquito incubators, as they absorb heat and trap rainwater, leaf litter and micro-organisms. Consequently, tyre piles can cause mosquito-borne diseases like encephalitis and malaria, amongst others. Spraying the piles with insecticides is costly and it's also almost impossible to reach the depths in the tyre piles where the mosquitoes reproduce.

Another constant threat is tyre pile fires. Because of the high flammable content in tyres, they burn intensely and are extremely difficult to extinguish. Applying water to tyre fires causes significant groundwater pollution and it's now recommended that ecologically, it's better to just let the tyres burn out rather than try to extinguish them. Tyre dumps can burn for months or years. A tyre dump fire in Tracy, California, had over eleven million tyres and burned for over two years before being extinguished. Another massive one last year was in Kuwait. It is believed that around ten million tyres fuelled the fire, which specialists struggled to control. Hundreds of firefighters, as well as soldiers and employees of the Kuwait Oil Company, took part in the efforts to extinguish the blaze. The fire was so great that it is reported that it could even be spotted by satellite cameras.

A new and alternative method of extinguishing a tyre fire is to use liquid nitrogen. A hose, insulated in order to keep the nitrogen sufficiently cold, expels a stream of liquid nitrogen through a nozzle, which is directed onto the burning tyres. When the liquid nitrogen hits the hot surface of the tyres, it immediately evaporates and expands by a factor of about nine hundred to form a ball of non-combustible nitrogen gas. That ball of gas immediately extinguishes the fire by preventing oxygen from reaching the burning tyres. The liquid nitrogen cannot explode nor cause any other hazardous actions. It simply extinguishes the fire. In addition as a further benefit, the temperature of the top of the burning tyres is immediately lowered, reducing the expulsion of any toxic gasses. Finally, using liquid nitrogen in this way produces nothing else, so the act of extinguishing the fire will not further contaminate the fire site.

If waste tyres are in good condition, they can be re-moulded and put back on the road as re-treads. However, if they're not in good condition, traditionally it's been hard to do something with end of life tyres. There is now though a new technology that exploits the nano particles in the rubber from recycled tyres to produce recycled tyre products. These include products designed for both indoor and outdoor use and for construction materials. Treating the products with colours and additives means they can be tailored to individual requirements. The end product is durable and prevents corrosion, which means that the applications are widespread. Once they have fulfilled their purpose, they can then be one hundred per cent recycled.

This new rubber material is extremely tough and is easy to clean. The products made from it are stronger than composite materials, and impervious to water and ultraviolet resistant, which makes the products perfect for floors, trailers, tiles, wood replacement for building, ports and extreme condition environments. Other uses include a children's playground, running tracks, artificial sports pitches, fuel for cement kilns, carpet underlay, equestrian arenas and flooring.

That is the end of section four. You will now have half a minute to check your answers.

(30-second gap)

This is the end of listening test twenty-five. In the IELTS test you would now have ten minutes to transfer your answers to the listening answer sheet.

Made in the USA
Coppell, TX
03 November 2020